Read to Succeed 2

Read to Succeed 2

ACADEMIC READING RIGHT FROM THE START

Roberto E. Robledo
Santa Barbara City College

Dolores Howard
Santa Barbara City College

Houghton Mifflin Company
Boston · New York

Publisher: Patricia A. Coryell
Director of ESL Publishing: Susan Maguire
Senior Development Editor: Kathy Sands Boehmer
Editorial Assistant: Evangeline Bermas
Senior Project Editor: Kathryn Dinovo
Senior Manufacturing Coordinator: Marie Barnes
Senior Marketing Manager: Annamarie Rice
Marketing Associate: Laura Hemrika

Cover image: CSA Images © 2003

Photo credits **p. 1:** © John Henley/CORBIS. **p. 2:** GDT/Getty Images. **p. 18:** Bruno De Hogues/Getty Images. **p. 34:** © Jackson Smith/ImageState-Pictor/PictureQuest. **p. 50:** © Robin Nelson/ PhotoEdit. **p. 69:** © CORBIS. **p. 70:** © CORBIS. **p. 90:** © Catherine Karnow/Woodfin Camp/PictureQuest. **p. 100:** © CORBIS. **p. 100:** © CORBIS. **p. 100:** AP/Wide World Photos. **p. 102:** AP/Wide World Photos. **p. 110:** Steve Satushek/Getty Images. **p. 133:** Ministère de la Culture/ CORBIS. **p. 151:** © Michael Newman/PhotoEdit. **p. 152:** AP/Wide World Photos. **p. 153:** AP/Wide World Photos. **p. 153:** AP/Wide World Photos. **p. 153:** AP/Wide World Photos. **p. 153:** AP/Wide World Photos. **p. 153:** AP/Wide World Photos. **p. 153:** AP/Wide World Photos. **p. 173:** © David Young Wolff/PhotoEdit. **p. 189:** © Helen King/CORBIS. **p. 208:** © Pete Saloutos/CORBIS

Printed in the U.S.A.

Library of Congress Control Number: 2002109662

ISBN: 0-618-32471-2

3456789-CRS-08 07 06 05

Contents

Unit 2: Readings in the Social Sciences

Reading and Skills Chart

Chapter	Reading Focus	Practical Focus	Grammar Focus	Expansion Activities
1. Going to the Movies	Comprehension: *Wh* and *Do* questions, scan words, true-false, main idea, complete a graphic map. Vocabulary: use words in context	Knowledge of movies as part of American culture	Simple present	Movie review (write about a favorite movie) Famous entertainers from around the world (match actors with country of origin)
2. Music Old and New	Comprehension: true-false, main idea, *Wh* and inferential questions Vocabulary: use words in context, find factual information, synonyms	Brief history of early musical instruments and contemporary musical forms	Simple present	Rhyme time (fill in rhyming words) My music (write about a favorite musician)
3. Our Changing Families	Comprehension: true-false, main idea, find factual information, complete a graphic map, *Wh* and inferential questions Vocabulary: use words in context, recognize definitions, write original sentences	Readings about different contemporary family units Reading charts and graphs (statistics about women and births)	Simple present	Family role play (write and present a dialogue) Letter to an adoptive child (write a letter about your family life)
4. Special People	Comprehension: true-false, main idea, *Wh* and inferential questions Vocabulary: antonyms, use words in context, comparative forms	Basic knowledge of learning disabilities and assistive technology	Review of present progressive, modal *can,* long and short comparatives	Answer questions about statistics (work with disabilities statistics) Crossword puzzle (complete a crossword puzzle using chapter vocabulary)
5. The First Americans	Comprehension: true-false, identify factual information, main idea, *Wh* and inferential questions Vocabulary: cloze paragraph, match word to definition/description, use context clues	United States early history and immigration Reading charts and graphs (immigration statistics)	Simple past (*to be* and regular and irregular verbs)	Word search (chapter-related words) Write your own story (write about how you came to the United States)
6. Americans and Their Leaders	Comprehension: main idea, identify factual information, true-false, *Wh* and inferential questions Vocabulary: cloze paragraph, synonyms, match words with definitions, modal auxiliaries	United States government, elections, and voter education	Modal auxiliaries, simple past	Register to vote (complete a voter registration form) Bingo (use chapter vocabulary words)

Reading and Skills Chart (continued)

Chapter	Reading Focus	Practical Focus	Grammar Focus	Expansion Activities
7. Continents and Population	Comprehension: main idea, true-false, identify factual information, *Wh* and inferential questions Vocabulary (use words in context, identify map locations, antonyms)	World geography and environment Reading charts and graphs (mountain ranges, rivers, population)	Review of simple present, present progressive, and simple past; superlative adjectives	Vocabulary game (give definitions) Research a country (choose a country to find information about)
8. Who Were Our Ancestors?	Comprehension: read a timeline, main idea, look for details, *Wh* and inferential questions, true-false Vocabulary: synonyms, categorize, words in context	General anthropology and human ancestors Reading charts and graphs (human life on Earth timeline)	Simple present and simple past	A letter from Homo habilis (describe prehistoric life) Crossword puzzle (complete a crossword puzzle using chapter vocabulary)
9. You Can't Control Mother Nature	Comprehension: main idea, matching, true/false, *Wh* and inferential questions Vocabulary: words in context, geographical words, prefixes *re-*, *pre-*, *un-*, synonyms, complete informational charts	Explanation of natural disasters and preparation for natural disasters Reading charts and graphs (emergency preparedness)	Simple present, simple past, review of modals	Write a story (write about a personal emergency or disaster) Natural disaster preparation (create emergency plan checklists)
10. Sharing or Stealing Music?	Comprehension: give opinions, true-false, main idea, *Wh* and inferential questions, write questions Vocabulary: true/false, use words in context, synonyms, prefixes *dis-* and *il-*	Uploading and downloading free music files from the Internet	Simple past and simple present	Check out those new legal music sites! (research and report on music Web sites) Conduct a survey (ask classmates and write results)
11. Diet, Exercise, and Fitness	Comprehension: main idea, true-false, find details, *Wh* and inferential questions Vocabulary: words in context, write original sentences, prefixes *in-* and *un-*	Exercise and eating right for good health Reading charts and graphs (statistics on obesity, inactivity, causes of and risks for death)	Past participle in the present perfect for regular verbs	Create a health commercial (with a group, make up and present a commercial about health and fitness) How healthy are your classmates? (survey classmates about their health and then present results)
12. Emergency Medical Measures	Comprehension: recognize summary, *Wh* and inferential questions, write questions, main idea, identify details, sequence Vocabulary: use words in context, synonyms, past progressive forms, review of prefixes *un-* and *in-*	EMT paramedics and organ donation Reading charts and graphs (drunk driving statistics)	Introduction to present perfect using irregular verbs, past progressive	Crossword puzzle (complete a crossword puzzle using chapter vocabulary) Organ donor ID card (complete a card)

Preface

Read to Succeed 2 is the second in a two-part series intended for low-intermediate ESL students. The varied readings introduce students to the reading process by using practical and interesting chapters on contemporary issues, social sciences, and science and technology. The text uses a communicative approach in each of the twelve similarly formatted chapters. Chapters contain, with some variation, prereading exercises with photos or illustrations, two readings, comprehension and vocabulary exercises, writing practice, practice with charts and graphs, expansion activities, and, where necessary, a focused grammar hint. The lesson topics have an academic yet manageable focus to develop students' success in reading, vocabulary, oral skills, listening skills, and writing skills through a variety of topics, graphics, and exercises.

Targeted Level

Read to Succeed 2 was written for low-intermediate ESL reading students taking second- or third-semester English as a Second Language reading classes (typically level 2 or 3 in a five-level ESL program). Book 2 is geared to the literate student who has taken at least a one-semester reading course or who has some English background and for whom learning English is essential for survival and success in school and in U.S. culture at large. Because *Read to Succeed 2* was written with the low-intermediate student in mind, the reading level does not outpace the typical grammar and writing level of a second- or third-semester student. The chapters also follow the typical grammar and writing sequence found in second- and third-semester ESL texts. There is a comprehensive vocabulary list at the end of each chapter and on the Web site.

Notable Features

Reading Readiness

- Each chapter begins with prereading exercises that focus students on the content of the reading and include photos or illustrations. These exercises help students acquire oral language facility and vocabulary in context before reading with the assistance of their teacher.
- The text gives students an opportunity to improve listening skills. The book's design gives the teacher opportunities to work on improving students' pronunciation through oral reading of words, sentences, and whole readings.
- Photos, illustrations, and charts and graphs make acquisition of vocabulary easier; thus, students can immediately associate photos, illustrations, and graphics with vocabulary.
- The vocabulary words in the beginning chapters are commonly used words in second- or third-semester reading texts, and much of this vocabulary

appears again in readings in later chapters. There are prefix and suffix exercises.

- Each chapter contains exercises for conversation in a group or pairs, which can later also be used as written homework assignments.

Reading Lessons

- Each reading uses carefully controlled syntax, grammar, and verb tenses.
- The three thematic units (twelve chapters) offer readings in several areas: movies, music, families, learning disabilities, history and immigration, political science, geography, anthropology, natural disasters, technology, diet and exercise, and medical emergencies.
- The twelve chapters maintain high student interest and do not overwhelm the low-intermediate student with grammar structures and vocabulary that are too difficult.
- The twelve chapters each have two reading selections. The first selection can be read by the teacher, if desired, to develop listening skills (or by the students aloud in class to work on pronunciation). A second reading selection can be used for silent reading. Both readings include comprehension and vocabulary exercises with clear directions, which may be completed as the teacher desires.
- Each chapter begins with prereading exercises and questions that focus students on the content of the reading and include photos or illustrations. These exercises develop student interest before the reading selection. The prereading pages lend themselves to overhead transparencies.
- All chapters include comprehension and vocabulary, writing, and conversation practice.
- The comprehension exercises include true-false, finding facts, main idea, simple inferential questions, sequence activities, and scanning for details.
- Vocabulary practice includes exercises in matching vocabulary with definition, fill-in, search, scanning, identifying synonyms and antonyms, multiple-choice questions, prefixes, suffixes, word forms, and conversation.
- Oral practice questions can be used in class in groups and pairs to give students opportunities for speaking in the classroom about a controlled topic. These questions can also be used for written homework.
- Writing practice is found in the form of fill-in, word-definition, and simple to compound sentence answers.
- The chapters are written in simple, clear, and understandable syntax, enhanced with photos, illustrations, and charts and graphs.
- The expansion activities for writing or vocabulary reinforcement at the end of each chapter provide follow-up activities to further explore the theme and to provide students with additional opportunities for oral, writing, and vocabulary practice.

- Audio program provides opportunities for listening practice with readings from the text as well as additional listening activities.
- The vocabulary list, whether on the Web site or the last page of the chapter, helps students review vocabulary, learn the parts of speech, and recognize word families. The Web site list includes vocabulary flashcards and other activities designed for additional reading and vocabulary practice.
- An appendix with U.S. and world maps complements the chapter contents.
- Almost all the chapters in *Read to Succeed 2* have been field-tested in the ESL Department's Credit ESL courses at Santa Barbara City College for the past fourteen years. The materials were found to be very successful for teachers and students in developing reading and vocabulary skills, and were at the correct level for students. We hope you will find them so as well.

Acknowledgments

We wish to thank:

Joann Kozyrev, for initially encouraging us to write this series
Susan Maguire, for her dynamic support and approval of this project
Kathy Sands-Boehmer, for her guidance in the development of this book
Kathleen Smith, for her wonderful suggestions and additions

We gratefully acknowledge our reviewers for their valuable input and suggestions:

Myrta Alvarez, University of Puerto Rico
Shannon Bailey, Austin Community College
Jane Berger, Solano Community College
Robert Ciapetta, Montgomery College
Gail Davis, College of Dupage
June Ohrnberger, Suffolk Community College
Helen Roland, Miami-Dade Community College
Lisa Stelle, Northern Virginia Community College
Tonia Trombetta, West Valley Community College
Olivia Villagra, Northlake College

Special thanks to our colleagues from the Disabled Student Programs and Services at Santa Barbara City College for their help, expertise, and willingness to share information and sources:

Laurie Vasquez and Geri Lewin

And special thanks to our families for being so patient while we wrote this book:

Maria Clara Garcia
Cuauhtémoc, Luna, Moctezuma, Quetzal, and Tláloc

Read to Succeed 2

UNIT 1

Readings in Contemporary Issues

CHAPTER 1

Going to the Movies

Reading 1 Everyone Likes a Movie!

Before You Read

▶EXERCISE 1 Discuss these questions with a partner or a small group.

1. What kind of movies do you like?
2. What are some good movies that you know?
3. Who are your favorite movie stars?

▶EXERCISE 2 Listen to your teacher read the sentences. Say the sentences after your teacher. Then match the sentences to the pictures. Write the correct letter next to the sentence.

Part 1

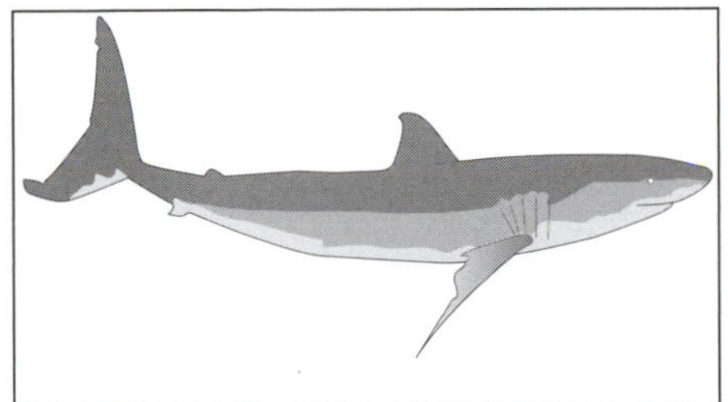

A.

B.

C.

D.

1. Many Web sites give information about movies. D
2. This animal scared people in one famous movie. ______
3. People cry at sad movies. ______
4. People laugh at funny movies. ______

Part 2

E.

F.

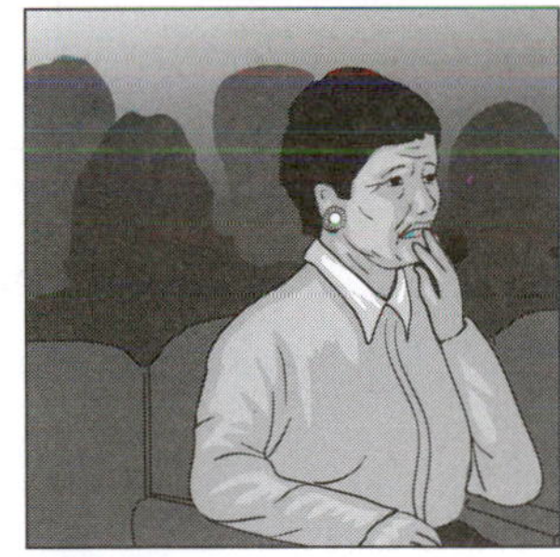

G.

H.

5. Some people go to the movies to see the attractive movie stars. ______
6. Car chases make movies interesting. ______
7. Some movies scare us. ______
8. Moviegoers wait in long lines for popular movies. ______

▶EXERCISE 3 Scan the reading for the correct vocabulary to complete each sentence.

1. *Film* is another word for ___*movie*___.
2. A funny movie is a ________.
3. A movie that makes a lot of money is a ________.
4. Happiness, sadness, fear, and excitement are ________.

Words from the Reading*

actor/actress	**fear**	**moneymaker**	**spy**
comedy	**laugh**	**silent**	

*Your teacher can help you understand these words and others listed at the end of the chapter and on the Web site at http://esl.college.hmco.com/students.

▶EXERCISE 4 Scan the reading and answer these questions.

1. What is one reason that people go to the movies? *People go to the movies to forget their problems.*
2. What are two examples of American movies that are romantic? ________
3. What kind of movie makes us laugh? ________
4. What two other types of movies are very popular? ________

Read to find out what people like about movies.

Everyone Likes a Movie!

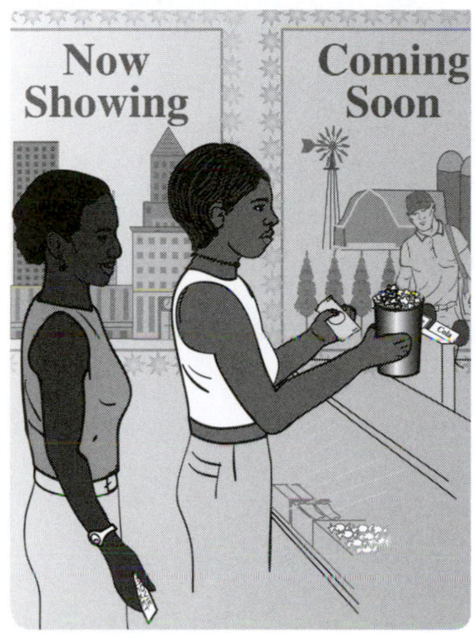

Do you like popcorn? A good movie? You're not alone! People today love movies. Why? Some go to the movies to forget their problems. They want to see lives that are different from theirs. Other people watch films because the stories are similar to their own lives. Probably one reason that people go to the movies is that movies have a big effect on our emotions. When we watch a movie, we feel happiness, sadness, fear, or excitement.

Perhaps you're the type that enjoys romantic movies. If that's the case, you know that the story is only a story, but the romance makes you happy or causes you to cry. Nowadays, romantic movies are sometimes called "chick flicks" because people think that mostly women appreciate romantic movies. In **reality,** though, both men and women get in line to buy tickets for romantic movies. *Titanic* (1997) and *Gone with the Wind* (1939), movies with a lot of romance, are among the most **profitable** movies in American movie history.

Watch an old silent film with Charlie Chaplin or a more recent comedy **release,** and you will see why movies that make us laugh are always popular. Laughter is the best medicine! Of course, it's not only the comedians that we go to see; the beautiful and handsome movie stars are another reason that people like the movies. One classic comedy, *Some Like It Hot* (1959), is funny and has attractive actors and actresses. One of them, Marilyn Monroe, is still very well-known today.

The movie *Psycho* (1960), by the director Alfred Hitchcock, doesn't scare audiences as much as it used to because now there are many scary movies, or thrillers. Most of them are big **moneymakers.** But watching them has an **impact** on us. After seeing *Jaws* (1975), some of us are afraid to swim in the ocean.

Other movie fans like action movies because they are exciting. Car chases, explosions, and "the good guys versus the bad guys" are exactly what many **moviegoers** are looking for. Look at how many James Bond 007 spy movies there are. Movies are very exciting and entertaining. So let's turn down the lights and **let the film roll!** It's not just the popcorn—it's the movies!

impact	the effect of something
let the film roll	start the movie
moneymaker	something that is successful in making money
moviegoer	a person who goes to see movies
profitable	producing a profit; moneymaking
reality	the quality of being real, not imaginary
release	something offered to the public

Comprehension

▸EXERCISE 5 Write T (true) or F (false) for each statement. Then discuss your answers with a classmate.

__F__ 1. People all love movies for the same reason.

_____ 2. The movie *Jaws* is not a scary movie for anyone.

_____ 3. A "chick flick" is a movie that only men like.

_____ 4. Attractive movie stars make movies that many people go to see.

_____ 5. Charlie Chaplin movies are funny.

_____ 6. People don't like excitement in movies.

_____ 7. The movie *Psycho* is a romantic film.

_____ 8. James Bond films are spy movies.

_____ 9. Car chases are popular with many moviegoers.

_____ 10. Movie directors don't make scary movies anymore.

▸EXERCISE 6 Find and underline the most important words or most important sentence that tells the topic of each paragraph in "Everyone Likes a Movie!" Then write your choice here.

Paragraph 1: *People today love movies.*

Paragraph 2: *romantic movies*

Paragraph 3: _____________________

Paragraph 4: _____________________

Paragraph 5: _____________________

▸EXERCISE 7 Complete information in each column for the types of movies listed.

Type of Movie	Famous Movie or Actor	Emotions We Feel
Romance	*Titanic, Gone with the Wind*	*happiness, sadness*
Comedy		
Thriller		
Action		

▸EXERCISE 8 Read the questions, and answer them orally with your teacher. Then answer them orally with a classmate. At home, write the answers for homework. Answer in complete sentences.

About the Reading

1. What do some people want to see in movies? ______________________

____

2. In what year was *Titanic* made? *Gone with the Wind*? ______________________

____

3. In what year was *Some Like It Hot* made? ______________________

____

4. What is different about some Charlie Chaplin movies from the movies of today?

____

5. When was *Psycho* made? ______________________

____

About You

6. Do you remember a movie that scared you? Explain. ______________________

____

7. What do you prefer—an action movie or a romantic movie? Why? ______________________

____

8. What movie stars make you laugh the most? ______________________

____

9. Do you agree that "Laughter is the best medicine"? Why or why not? ______________________

____

10. Do you prefer to stand in line at the movie theater to see a new release, or do you wait to see it later? ______________________

____

Vocabulary Practice

▸EXERCISE 9 Complete each sentence with a word from the box.

film	fan	~~impact~~	silent	well-known	comedian
effect	profitable	laugh	fear	moviegoers	spy

1. Learning English has had a big ___*impact*___ on my life.
2. The teacher doesn't want the children to talk while they are working. She wants them to be ________________.
3. This is a great ________________. I like this movie.
4. You make me laugh. You are a ________________.
5. That actor is not very ________________. He isn't very popular yet.
6. Loud noise has a bad ________________ on him. It makes him feel bad.
7. I'm a ________________ of old movies. I watch them all the time.
8. Don't ________________ at him! It's not funny!
9. Movies that are moneymakers are very ________________ for the directors and actors.
10. Some people have a ________________ of sharks.
11. She has a special, secret job with the government. She is a ________________.
12. Many ________________ were in love with Marilyn Monroe.

Reading 2 The World of the Movies

Before You Read

▸EXERCISE 10 Complete each sentence.

1. A movie that is similar to a cartoon is ___*animated*___.
2. Part two of a movie is called a ________________.
3. Movie ________________ write about the good and bad qualities of a movie.

Words from the Reading*

animated	**plot**	**audience**	**science fiction**
critic	**sequel**	**fascinating**	**special effect**
loyal	**spectacular**		

*Your teacher can help you understand these words and others listed at the end of the chapter and on the Web site at http://esl.college.hmco.com/students.

▶EXERCISE 11 Scan the reading to answer these questions.

1. What are some things that moviegoers enjoy about movies besides the story?

   special effects, movie stars' hairstyles and clothes

2. When was the first full-length animated movie made?

   ____

3. What do people often buy after they see a movie they like?

   ____

4. What do moviemakers often make when people really like a movie?

   ____

Read to find out about much more than just the movies.

The World of Movies

Traditional stories often begin with the phrase "Once upon a time" and often end with the words "The end." Movies have a beginning and an end, too, but moviegoers pay attention to more than just how the movie begins and ends. From special effects to movie stars' hairstyles and clothes, audiences find many fascinating things to enjoy about movies.

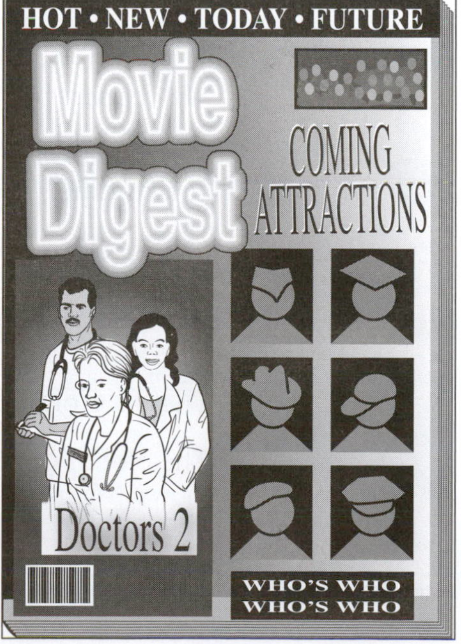

Today there are always new movies with spectacular special effects that make us ask, "How did they do that?" In 1937 *Snow White and the Seven Dwarves* was the first **full-length** animated movie, something new for that time. *Star Wars* (1977) is a special-effect science fiction movie with many loyal fans. Movie critics sometimes say that the special effects in films today seem more important to some people than the plot, or story, of the movie or the quality of the acting.

After they see a movie they like, people want to imitate and remember it. Some fans copy the clothes and hairstyles they see in the films and buy magazines about movies and the world of superstar actors. **Gossip** about celebrities sells very well! When customers by food, fast-food restaurants give away toys that depict popular movie actors or objects from movies. Movie **posters** and special editions of movies on videos and DVDs are often **collector's items.**

All this excitement about a movie can continue for a long time. When movies are very popular, filmmakers create sequels, or movies that continue the story of previous movies. Of course, there are thousands of Web sites for fans of old and new movies to share information and comments about their favorite movies. If you are a big fan of a particular movie, you can get into a **chat room** with other fans of the same movie and discuss your favorite parts and even write your own **movie reviews.** With all these possibilities for getting involved, movies are much more than just what we see at the movie theater.

chat room	a place to carry on an electronic conversation
collector's item	something people collect that has a particular value to them
full-length	of normal or standard length
gossip	talk of little importance or value, often involving rumors of people and their personal affairs
movie review	a report that discusses a movie and judges its worth
poster	a large notice, announcement, or picture displayed

Comprehension

▸EXERCISE 12 Write T (true) or F (false) for each statement. Then discuss your answers with a classmate.

__F__ 1. Traditional stories often begin with the words "The end."

_____ 2. Moviegoers buy books, magazines, and toys about movies.

_____ 3. The movie *Snow White and the Seven Dwarves* was made in a style that was old at that time.

_____ 4. Movie reviewers sometimes criticize the special effects in films.

_____ 5. Gossip about superstar actors and actresses is one of the reasons that movie fans buy magazines about movies.

_____ 6. There are only a few Web sites about movies.

_____ 7. The plot of the movie is the special effects of the movie.

_____ 8. Movie posters are very popular.

_____ 9. *Star Wars* is a comedy film.

_____ 10. Some fans imitate the hairstyles they see in the movies.

▶EXERCISE 13 Circle the letter of the main idea for each paragraph.

Paragraph 1:

a. Traditional stories begin with the phrase "Once upon a time."
b. Movies have a beginning and an end.
(c.) Moviegoers are excited about many aspects of movies.

Paragraph 2:

a. *Snow White* and *Star Wars* have special effects.
b. Special effects make movies popular.
c. Only new movies have special effects.

Paragraph 3:

a. People change their hair after they see a movie.
b. Moviegoers don't stop thinking about a movie after they see it.
c. There are Web sites about movies.

Paragraph 4:

a. Sequels are movies that continue the story of previous movies.
b. Chat rooms are interesting places to meet new friends.
c. You can continue the excitement of your favorite film in many ways.

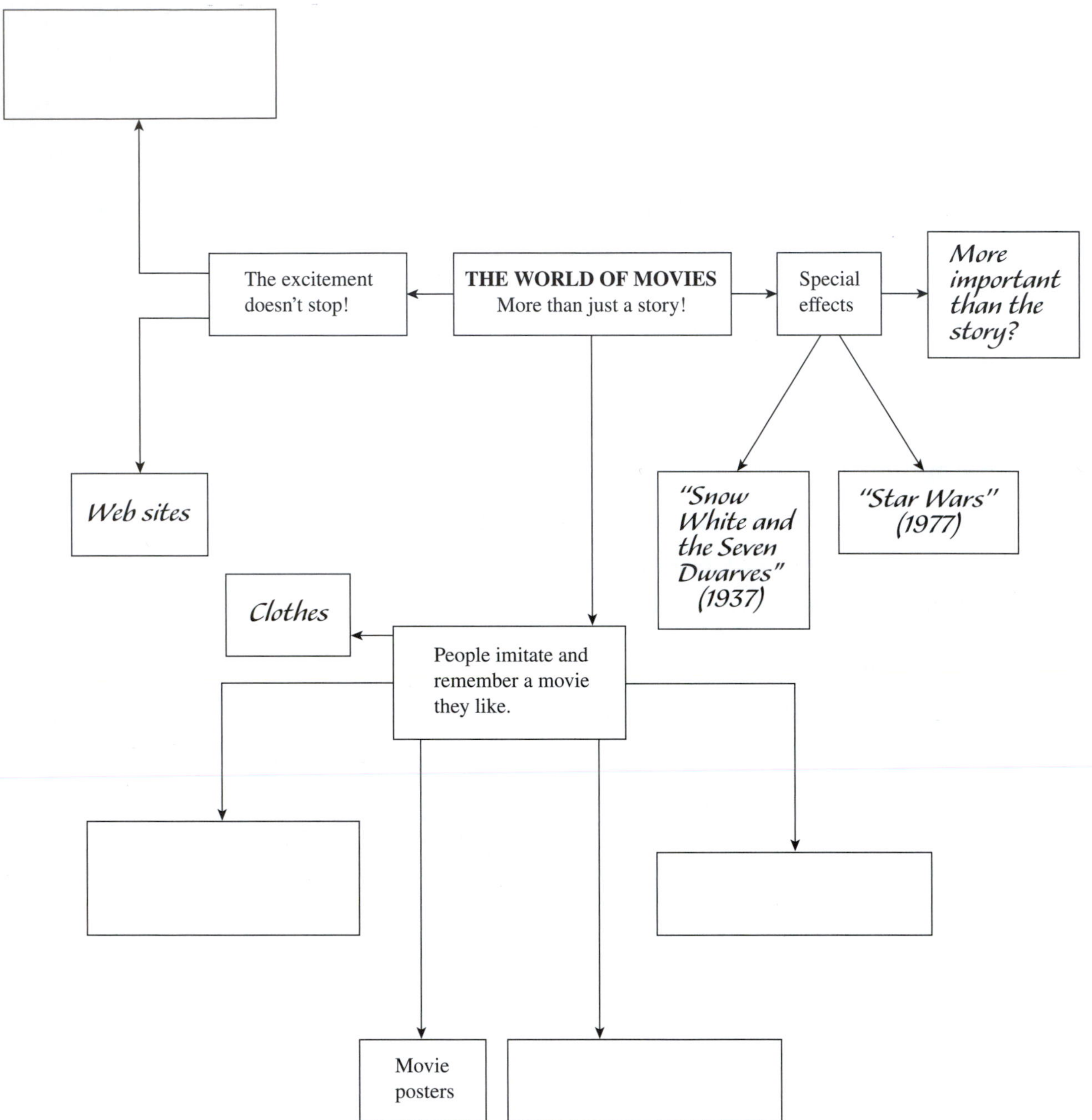
The excitement doesn't stop!
THE WORLD OF MOVIES
More than just a story!
Special effects
More important than the story?
Web sites
"Snow White and the Seven Dwarves" (1937)
"Star Wars" (1977)
Clothes
People imitate and remember a movie they like.
Movie posters

▸EXERCISE 15 Answer the questions orally with your teacher. Then answer the questions orally with a classmate. At home, write the answers for homework. Answer in complete sentences.

About the Reading

1. How do traditional stories often begin? *Traditional stories often begin with the phrase "Once upon a time."*
2. What was the first full-length animated movie? ______________________
3. What kind of movie was *Star Wars*? ______________________
4. What do movie critics sometimes say about special effects? ______________________
5. What things do people buy after they see a movie? ______________________
6. What makes the magazines about movie stars sell so well? ______________________
7. What can you do in a movie chat room? ______________________

About You

8. Do you go to a movie theater, or do you wait to see a movie on DVD or video? ______________________
9. What do you enjoy most about a movie—the plot, the acting, or the special effects? ______________________
10. What movies do you know that have sequels? ______________________

Vocabulary Practice

▸EXERCISE 16 Complete each sentence with a word from the box.

A.

action	gossip	laugh	moviegoers	romantic
~~swim~~	real	loyal	scare	audiences

1. Victor's daughter wants to ____*swim*____ in the pool.
2. This story is not ________________. Someone invented this story.
3. When Jack and his friends are together, they ________________ and have fun.
4. Many ________________ want to see a movie the first day it comes out.
5. This love story is very ________________.
6. I don't like horror films. They ________________ me.
7. Teresa wants to see a movie with a lot of ________________. She likes exciting movies.
8. My friend is always there to help me and support me. She is very ________________.
9. I don't want to hear ________________ about other people. Most of it is stories that aren't true.
10. The show was boring, and the ________________ didn't like it.

B.

animated	science fiction	excitement	full-length	spectacular
sequel	hairstyles	Web sites	critics	special effects

1. The Internet has millions of ________________.
2. Cartoons are ________________ movies.

3. I really liked the movie *The Godfather,* and now I want to see the ________________, *The Godfather II.*
4. Everyone pays attention to movie stars' ________________ and clothes.
5. Yuri really likes the ________________ of an adventure story.
6. ________________ are people who watch a movie and tell their opinion about it.
7. Technology makes ________________ possible.
8. Fantastic! The view of the ocean is ________________ today.
9. This isn't a ________________ movie. It lasts only 13 minutes.
10. ________________ movies use science and imagination.

Expansion Activities

► **Activity 1 Movie Review** *Write about your favorite movie. What kind of movie is it? Action? Drama? Comedy? A romantic movie? Who are the main (most important) actors? What happens in the movie? Why do you like this movie? Share your movie review with a partner.*

Here is an example of a movie review:

If you're looking for romance, adventure, attractive actors, and a beautiful story, I recommend the movie *Casablanca,* made in 1942. It's a wonderful film that is still popular today. The acting is excellent; Humphrey Bogart and Ingrid Bergman are outstanding! The cinematography is beautiful, and the song made famous by this film, "As Time Goes By," is unforgettable. The story involves a love triangle and does not have a typical "Hollywood" ending. The story takes place during World War II in Casablanca, Morocco. Ilsa (Ingrid Bergman) and her husband, Victor Laszlo (Paul Henreid), come to Rick's Café in Casablanca. The owner of the café is Rick Blaine (Humphrey Bogart), a man that Ilsa once loved very much. The political situation of the time also makes the story very interesting. I loved this black-and-white film very much—it's a movie to see again and again.

► Activity 2 Famous Entertainers from Around the World *Many famous entertainers bring their talents to the United States. Match each entertainer with his or her country of origin.*

1. Andy Garcia, actor ______
2. Nicole Kidman, actress ______
3. Liam Neeson, actor ______
4. Salma Hayek, actress ______
5. Arnold Schwarzenegger, actor ______
6. Mikhail Baryshnikov, dancer ______
7. Midori, violinist ______
8. Jennifer Lopez, singer and actress ______
9. Jackie Chan, actor ______
10. Catherine Zeta-Jones, actress ______

a. China
b. Australia
c. Cuba
d. Austria
e. Wales
f. United States
g. Japan
h. Ireland
i. Russia
j. Mexico

► Activity 3 Favorite Actor or Actress *Now think of your favorite actor or actress. What questions would you like to ask him or her?*

Name of actor/actress: ______________________________

Questions you would like to ask him/her:

1. *What was the best movie you have acted in?*
2. ______________________________
3. ______________________________
4. ______________________________
5. ______________________________

Vocabulary List

Adjectives

action
adventure
animated
attractive
classic
famous
fascinating
full-length
funny
handsome
horror
loyal
popular
profitable
real
romantic
secret
silent
spectacular
spy
traditional
well-known

Adverbs

obviously
possibly

Nouns

acting
action
actor
actress
audience
celebrity/celebrities
chat room
collector's item
comedian
comedy/comedies
critic
director
emotion
excitement
fear
film
filmmaker
gossip
hairstyle
impact
magazine
moneymaker
moviegoer
movie review
plot
popcorn
poster
reality
release
science fiction
sequel
special effect
theater
toy
Web site

Verbs

buy
criticize
cry
depict
enjoy
forget
imitate
know
last
laugh
let the film roll
pay attention
roll
scare
show
watch

If you want to review vocabulary and complete additional activities related to this chapter, go to the *Read to Succeed 2* Web site at http://esl.college.hmco.com/students.

CHAPTER 2

Music Old and New

Reading 1 Early Music

Before You Read

►EXERCISE 1 Discuss these questions with a partner or a small group.

1. What is the first music you remember from when you were a child?
2. When do you listen to music?
3. What traditional music does your country have?

▶EXERCISE 2 Listen to your teacher read the sentences. Say the sentences after your teacher. Then match the sentences to the pictures. Write the correct letter next to the sentence.

Can you guess what instruments these are?

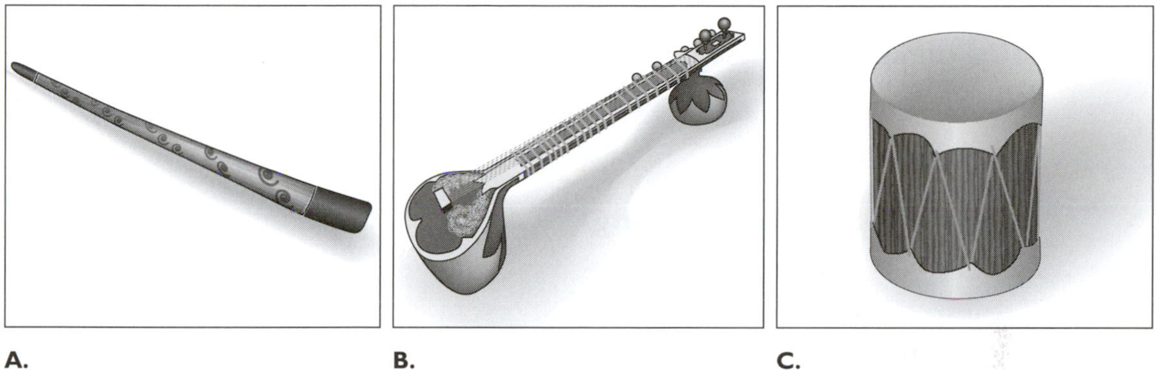

A. **B.** **C.**

These are things that people use to make musical instruments. What are they?

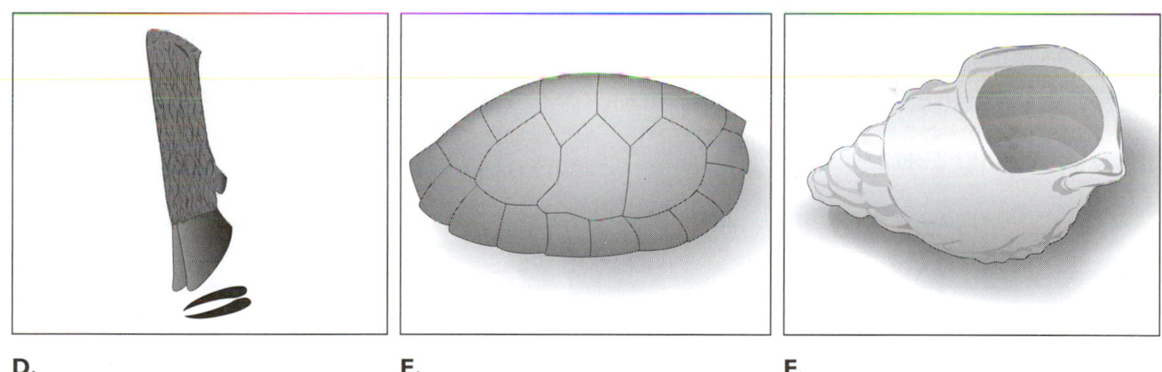

D. **E.** **F.**

1. This instrument with strings comes from India. ___B___
2. This instrument was once the home of an animal with four legs. ______
3. This is an Australian instrument made of rotten wood. ______
4. This is an animal's foot. ______
5. People make these from animals' skins. ______
6. This was an animal's home. ______

▶EXERCISE 3 Write a short answer for each of the following questions.

1. Are the roots of a tree the beginning or the end of the tree? *the beginning*
   Are the roots of music the beginning or the end of music? ______
2. The violin and the guitar are string instruments. What is another string instrument?
   ______
3. The trumpet and the saxophone are wind instruments. What is another wind instrument? ______

Words from the Reading*

chant	**root**
drum	**string**
musician	**wind**

*Your teacher can help you understand these words and others listed at the end of the chapter and on the Web site at http://esl.college.hmco.com/students.

▶EXERCISE 4 Scan the reading and answer these questions.

1. What did early people use music for? *They used music for hunting and working and honoring their gods.*
2. Where were the first musicians from? ______
   ______
3. What kind of materials do people use for instruments? ______
   ______

Read to find out about early music and musical instruments.

Early Music

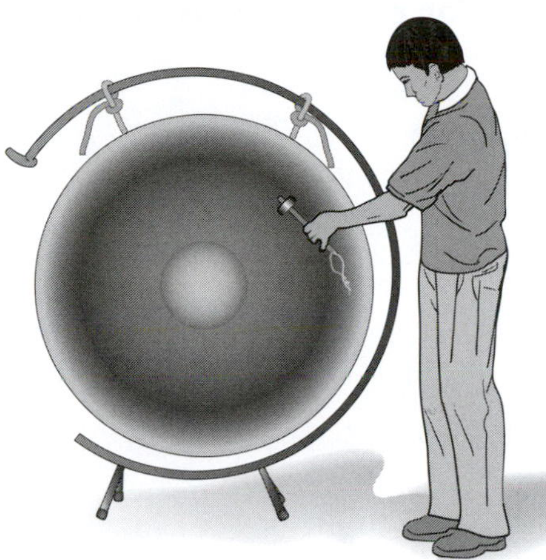

"Wait! Listen! There's my favorite song! Turn it up! What a great song." When we hear a favorite song, it seems like the best music in the world. Most of us feel that the music that we prefer is the greatest music ever. But today's music has roots in the music of the past. Let's take a look at the beginnings of music. Let's go back thousands of years to music in its earliest forms.

Who are the first musicians? What are the first chants or songs? What are the first instruments? Early humans are the first dancers, singers, and musicians. Their music is for hunting and working and honoring their gods. African tribal music is one of the first musical forms. Drums, which are an example of a percussion instrument, are important in African tribal music.

Time passes, and people make other instruments from natural materials. In the Americas, people use conch **shells** or **rattles** made from wood or parts of animals, including deer **hooves** and turtle shells. People living in Australia create the "didgeridoo," a wind instrument, from **rotten** wood. The **wood** is rotten because of termites, which eat the wood.

As the years go by, new instruments appear. In Southeast Asia, musicians play music on **gongs,** another percussion instrument, made from metals. The musicians hit the gongs with small hammers. In India, the sitar, a string instrument, produces beautiful sounds. The modern violin possibly has its **origins** in Asia and Europe. We find the guitar in Spain five hundred or more years ago.

Today, we still hear music that uses these instruments and many others. We listen to new songs and old favorites, as well as **remakes** of old songs with different artists and the latest technology. New technology produces new sounds for us to enjoy. Music is constantly changing, but a big part of the music that we **appreciate** today comes from the earliest forms of music.

appreciate	to recognize the worth, quality, or value of
gong	a saucer-shaped metal disk that produces a loud ringing tone when struck
hoof	the whole foot or tough, horny covering on the lower part of the foot of certain mammals, such as horses, cattle, deer, and pigs
origin	source or beginning
rattle	a device or object that makes a noise when shaken
remake	a thing that is made again
rotten	decayed or decomposed
shell	the usually hard outer covering of certain animals, such as mollusks, insects, and turtles
wood	the tough fibrous substance beneath the bark of trees and shrubs

Comprehension

▸EXERCISE 5 Write T (true) or F (false) for each statement. Then discuss your answers with a classmate.

__T__ 1. The first musicians play music for their gods.

_____ 2. Early humans never dance.

_____ 3. The first music is probably from Africa.

_____ 4. African music doesn't use drums.

_____ 5. People make the first instruments from plastic.

_____ 6. Conch shells are popular in the Americas.

_____ 7. In Australia, termites eat wood, and people make instruments from the wood.

_____ 8. Gongs are wood instruments.

_____ 9. Sitars are not common now.

_____ 10. Music is always the same.

▸EXERCISE 6 Circle the letter of the main idea for each paragraph.

Paragraph 1:

a. Modern music is the best.
b. Everyone has a favorite type of music.
(c.) The music we enjoy today comes from the past.

Paragraph 2:

a. The first humans have no interest in music.
b. The first humans have various reasons for playing music.
c. The first humans believe in gods.

Paragraph 3:

a. People make instruments from natural materials.
b. Drums are everywhere in the world.
c. Some people study music.

Paragraph 4:

a. In the Americas, people use conch shells.

b. People all over the world use many kinds of instruments.

c. People today still enjoy the sitar.

Paragraph 5:

a. Remakes of old songs are popular.

b. New technology is better than early music.

c. We still hear the music of early instruments as well as modern instruments.

►EXERCISE 7 Match the two parts of each sentence.

1. Early humans had music for __e__
2. The first musicians ______
3. Drums ______
4. People created instruments ______
5. The didgeridoo ______
6. Termites ______
7. Gongs are instruments ______
8. Musicians hit ______
9. Music is ______
10. Deer hooves and turtle shells ______

a. are parts of animals.
b. are insects that eat wood.
c. from natural materials.
d. gongs with small hammers.
e. hunting, working, and religion.
f. is from Australia.
g. made from metal.
h. still changing.
i. are important in African music.
j. were probably African people.

Extra "musical" work:

1. What other wind instruments do you know? ______________________________

____

2. What other percussion instruments do you know? ______________________________

____

3. What other string instruments do you know? ______________________________

____

▶EXERCISE 8 Read the questions and answer them orally with your teacher. Then answer them orally with a classmate. At home, write the answers for homework. Answer in complete sentences.

About the Reading

1. What is an early wind instrument? *An early wind instrument is the didgeridoo.*
2. What continent is the didgeridoo from? ____________
3. What do termites eat? ____________
4. What do musicians use to play gongs? ____________
5. What type of instrument is the sitar? ____________
6. How old is the guitar? ____________

About You

7. What is your favorite instrument? ____________
8. What instruments are used in traditional music in your country? ____________
9. How is traditional music in your country different from modern music? ____________
10. Which instrument would you like to learn to play? ____________

Vocabulary Practice

▸EXERCISE 9 Complete each sentence with a word from the box.

early	rotten	ants	metal	~~instrument~~
shells	chants	tribal	wind	deer

1. A guitar is an example of an *instrument*.
2. I see the trees moving outside. The ________________ is very strong today.
3. ________________ people lived in tribes.
4. A car has many ________________ parts.
5. I like to look for ________________ at the beach.
6. I see a beautiful ________________ eating near the water.
7. People sing ________________ with no music.
8. Some ________________ are eating our food.
9. The ________________ humans were the first humans.
10. When food is ________________, you don't eat it.

▸EXERCISE 10 Complete the information in each column for the instruments listed.

Name	Type	Material	Origin	Still Used Today?
Conch shell	*Wind*	*Animal's shell*	*Americas*	*Yes*
Didgeridoo				
Drum				
Gong				
Guitar				
Sitar				

Reading 2 Contemporary Music in the United States

Before You Read

▶EXERCISE 11 Write a short answer for each of the following questions.

1. Blue is a color and also a word that can mean "sad." What kind of music do you think blues music is? ______________________________

____

2. The words *bat, cat,* and *hat* are words that rhyme. What do you think *rhyme* means?

____

3. *Diversity* and *variety* have similar meanings. What do these words mean? __________

____

▶EXERCISE 12 Scan the reading and answer these questions.

1. What are some types of music in the United States? *blues, jazz, country*
2. Where is jazz music originally from? ____________
3. What do people think about freedom in music? ______________________________

____

Words from the Reading*

contemporary	**lyric**	**controversial**	**rap**
cowboy	**rhyme**	**diversity**	**theme**

*Your teacher can help you understand these words and others listed at the end of the chapter and on the Web site at http://esl.college.hmco.com/students.

Read to find out about a variety of music that is popular now in the United States.

Contemporary Music in the United States

Modern American music is rich in its variety of forms, styles, and instruments. A complete encyclopedia of American music is a small library! By just looking at a few types of American music, we can see much diversity.

Blues music, which goes back to the 1860s, has African American roots. Blues singers often sing of sad themes: feelings of **loneliness** or **hunger,** or being far away from home. The banjo and the **washboard** were **common** instruments in early blues music. The harmonica, guitar, and piano are some of the many other instruments used in blues.

Jazz has its beginnings in the 1890s in New Orleans. The musical contributions of people from many parts of the world came together in this port on the Mississippi River to create the early versions of jazz. The saxophone is a common instrument in many jazz bands. Now jazz comes in many forms and is popular in the United States and many other countries.

The fiddle is a common instrument in early country music, but today we hear many kinds of instruments in country music, especially the guitar. Cowboy movies in the 1930s and 1940s helped to make country music very popular.

Elvis Presley, Little Richard, the Beatles—bad influences? We know the bad opinions that some people had of electric guitar-playing rock musicians in the 1950s and 1960s, but sometimes we hear the same **criticisms** today about rock and other types of music. However, rock music is now one of the most popular types of music in the world.

Rap music has its origins in New York in the early 1970s. Rap uses a lot of rhyming. Rhymes are words that sound the same. Many young people like the beat in rap music. Often, the lyrics are about violence, sex, and drugs. Some people worry that rap music might be another bad influence on young people.

People have different ideas about freedom in music nowadays. Some of the public wants more control over the lyrics in songs and on music videos on TV. They protest the content of music and music videos. Some people don't like the **treatment** of women and sexual themes in some modern music. They say that these themes are harmful for young children and adolescents. Other music fans and musicians argue that freedom of expression is more important. They say that people don't have to buy CDs and music videos if they don't like them. Many young people say that this music is not offensive to them.

Like all music, contemporary American music causes people to sing, dance, smile, and cry. American music is sometimes controversial, but it shows us the diversity of American culture.

common	found often and in many places; usual
criticism	an expression of disapproval
hunger	strong desire or need for food
loneliness	sadness at being alone
treatment	the way of dealing with a person or thing
washboard	a rough board used for washing clothes and sometimes used as a percussion instrument

Comprehension

▸EXERCISE 13 Write T (true) or F (false) for each statement.

__T__ 1. Modern music uses different forms, styles, and instruments.

_____ 2. The washboard is an instrument that is new to blues music today.

_____ 3. We can hear country music in cowboy movies of the 1930s and 1940s.

_____ 4. Musicians often played the saxophone in early country music.

_____ 5. The saxophone is very popular for jazz fans.

_____ 6. The Beatles and Elvis Presley were popular with everyone.

_____ 7. Rap music started in New York.

_____ 8. There are many different cultural contributions to music.

_____ 9. Everyone is happy about the lyrics in modern music.

_____ 10. For some people, bad words are part of freedom of expression.

▸EXERCISE 14 Complete each sentence to give one important idea from each paragraph.

Paragraph 1: There are many *different kinds of modern American music.*

Paragraph 2: Blues music _______________.

Paragraph 3: Jazz music _______________.

Paragraph 4: Country music _______________.

Paragraph 5: When people talk about rock music, _______________.

Paragraph 6: Rap music is sometimes controversial because _______________.

Paragraph 7: People have different opinions about _______________.

Paragraph 8: Modern music is the story of _______________.

▸EXERCISE 15

A. Match the two parts of each sentence.

1. Blues songs __a__
2. American music ____
3. Jazz music comes from ____
4. Music makes us ____
5. Some people think that ____
6. Rap music was first popular ____
7. Some music fans don't have a problem ____
8. Some people are offended by ____
9. The fiddle was common ____
10. There are different views about ____

a. often have sad themes.
b. in New York.
c. in early country music.
d. rock music is a bad influence on young people.
e. is very diverse.
f. a port city on the Mississippi.
g. freedom in music.
h. the sexual themes in music.
i. with modern CDs and music videos.
j. smile, cry, dance, and sing.

B. Complete the timeline for the history of American music with other types of music that you know.

Years	1860s	1890s	1930s & 1940s	1950s & 1960s	1970s
Types of Music	Blues				

▸EXERCISE 16 Read the questions and answer them orally with your teacher. Then answer the questions orally with a classmate. At home, write the answers for homework. Answer in complete sentences.

About the Reading

1. Why is an encyclopedia of American music a small library? *An encyclopedia of American music is a small library because there are so many kinds of American music.*
2. What is blues music? ______________________________
3. When was jazz first popular? ______________________________
4. What instrument was common in early country music? ______________________________
5. Why do some people protest about modern music? ______________________________
6. What do people say about the sexual themes and treatment of women in some modern music? ______________________________

About You

7. Who is your favorite musician? Why is he or she your favorite? ______________________________
8. Do you think we need more control over lyrics and music videos? Why? ______________________________
9. When do you listen to music? ______________________________
10. What are some types of dance that are popular in your country? ______________________________

Vocabulary Practice

▸EXERCISE 17 Write a synonym from "Contemporary Music in the United States" for each word or phrase. A synonym is the same or similar word.

1. topics (paragraph 2) ____________________
2. variety (paragraph 1) ____________________
3. modern (title) ____________________
4. liberty (paragraph 7) ____________________
5. limits (paragraph 7) ____________________
6. words in songs (paragraph 7) ____________________
7. speak against (paragraph 7) ____________________
8. admirers (paragraph 7) ____________________
9. dangerous (paragraph 7) ____________________
10. not kind (paragraph 7) ____________________

▸EXERCISE 18 Complete the information in each column for the instruments listed.

Type of Music	Common Instruments	Other Information
Blues		
Country	*Fiddle, guitar*	*Popular in cowboy movies in 1930s and 1940s*
Jazz		
Rap		
Rock		

Expansion Activities

▸ **Activity 1 Rhyme Time** *A lot of music uses rhyme. Two words rhyme when the endings of both words sound the same. Write a word that rhymes with each of these words:*

bat ____________ run ____________

take ____________ red ____________

car ____________ note ____________

bad ____________ shoe ____________

rock ____________ white ____________

Think of other pairs of words that rhyme, and write them here:

____________ ____________ ____________ ____________ ____________ ____________

____________ ____________ ____________ ____________ ____________ ____________

▸ **Activity 2 My Music** *Bring a picture of your favorite musician or musical group to class. If you don't have a picture, draw one. Explain to a group of students or to the class why you like this singer or group. Use these or other words:*

This is ____________________ (name). He/She/They ____________________ (is/are) my favorite because he/she/they ____________________ (is/are) ____________________ (beautiful/talented/great singer/excellent piano player/handsome). This singer/group is also special because ____________________ (has a good voice/dances well/is a good person). I listen to this music when I am ____________________ (sad/happy/studying/at a party).

Finally, hum (sing with no words) one line from a song by your favorite singer or group. See if the class can guess the title.

Vocabulary List

Adjectives

common
contemporary
controversial
favorite
metal
modern
natural
offensive
rap
rotten
string
tribal
wind

Adverbs

constantly
originally

Nouns

adolescent
chant
content
cowboy
criticism
deer
diversity
drum
fiddle
foot
freedom of expression
gong
hammer
hoof/hooves
hunger
instrument
loneliness
lyric
musician
origin
rap
rattle
remake
root
saxophone
shell
skin
string
termite
theme
treatment
turtle
washboard
wind
wood

Verbs

appreciate
create
dance
hit
honor
play (music)
protest
rhyme
sing

If you want to review vocabulary and complete additional activities related to this chapter, go to the *Read to Succeed 2* Web site at http://esl.college.hmco.com/students.

CHAPTER 3

Our Changing Families

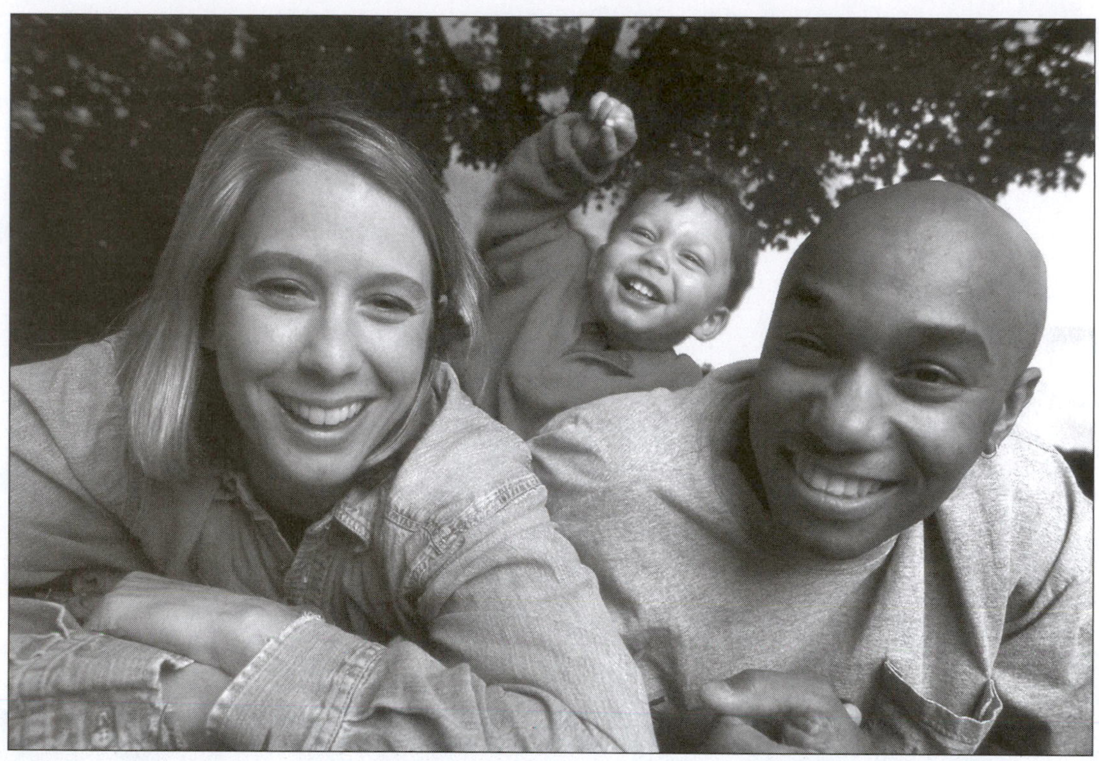

Reading 1 Today's American Families

Before You Read

▶**EXERCISE 1 Discuss these questions with a partner or a small group.**

1. What is the typical family for you?
2. What do you know about adopted children in your country? Is adoption common in your country?
3. What is important for a family to be successful?

Reading Charts and Graphs

▶EXERCISE 2

Part I

A. Study the statistics about women and babies.

There were 60.9 million women 15–44 years old in the United States in 2000.*

Women who did not have a child in 2000*	56.1 million
Women who gave birth in 2000*	4.1 million
Single women who gave birth in 2000**	1.2 million
Girls 15–19 years old who had a child in 2000 (4.1% of all births)*	166,411

*National Center for Health Statistics, 2000.
**U.S. Census, 2000.

B. Answer these questions with a partner or a small group.

1. How many women did not have a child in 2000? *56.1 million*
2. How many women had babies in 2000? ______
3. How many unmarried women had babies in 2000? ______
4. How many teenagers had babies in 2000? ______
5. What other information do you want to know about women and babies in the United States? ______
6. What difficulties do single parents have in raising their children? ______
7. How are U.S. families different from families in your country? ______

Part 2

A. Study the statistics about births by ethnic group.

All Live Births (Over 4 Million) in 2000 in the United States by Ethnic Group*

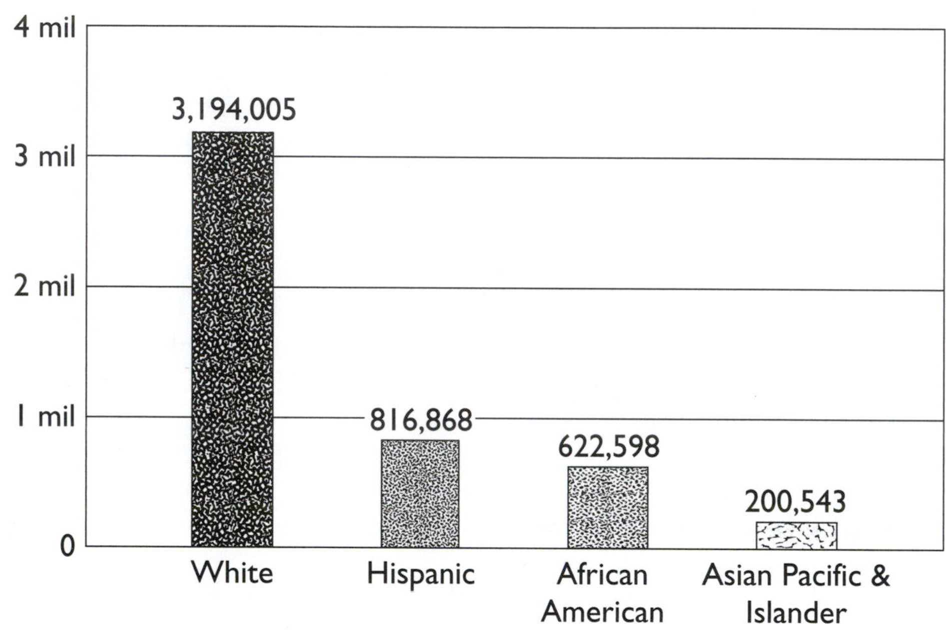

*National Center for Health Statistics, 2000.

B. Answer these questions with a partner or a small group.

1. Which ethnic group had the highest number of babies? ____white____
2. Which group had the lowest number of babies? ______________
3. How many Hispanic births were there in 2000? ______________
4. There are more African Americans than Hispanics, but there were more Hispanic babies in 2000. Why do you think this was true?

   ____

5. What is the total number of babies born in 2000 in the United States in the groups shown? ______________

▶EXERCISE 3 Scan the reading for this vocabulary and then match the term with the definition.

1. blended family __c__
2. adopt ______
3. foster parent ______
4. birth children ______

a. a person who gives parental care to a child not legally related
b. to take legal responsibility for a person new to the family
c. a family with children from different marriages
d. children born naturally to a parent

Words from the Reading*

adoption	**couple**	**birth children**	**foster parent**
blended family	**sibling**	**challenge**	

*Your teacher can help you understand these words and others listed at the end of the chapter and on the Web site at http://esl.college.hmco.com/students.

▶EXERCISE 4 Scan the reading and answer these questions.

1. Why do we see more children from different family units coming together in one family? *We see more children from different family units coming together in one family because of the high divorce rate.*
2. How are adoptive families now different from in the past? ______________________

   ____
3. What does foster parenting offer children? ______________________

   ____

Read about the variety of families in America today.

Today's American Families

Are you thinking of starting a family someday in the future? Or do you have children already? Even if you don't have children, you probably know people with families in the United States, and you probably **recognize** that American families come in many different shapes and sizes.

Perhaps the biggest difference in American families today from traditional families is the number of "blended families," or families with children from different marriages. With high divorce rates, we see large numbers of couples in their second marriage, and this means that children from different family units come together into one family. This blending presents challenges for everyone. Just because two people love each other doesn't mean their children are happy to be together or to have a new parent. "You're not my mom" or "You're not my dad," the children sometimes say to their new **stepmother** or **stepfather.** The situation is especially difficult when there are teenagers wanting independence at a time that the family needs to **unite.** However, many stepfamilies are finding that they can make their blended families work. The members of stepfamilies can learn a lot from one another. Blended families need to work hard at creating respect for all members and treating family members fairly.

Although adoption is not new, adoptive families have a different face than in the past. Now it is more common to see adoptive families with both birth children and adoptive children. Parents who already have birth children have experience that helps them with being adoptive parents, and the children they adopt come into families where siblings are waiting for them. However, **adjusting** to a new family is never completely easy, especially when an older child is adopted. On the other hand, one of the advantages of adopting an older child is that the child brings memories, experiences, and sometimes language and culture that are new to the family adopting him or her. This same situation can be challenging, too.

Foster parenting provides temporary homes for children in a crisis situation. This type of parenting is usually assigned by agencies of local government, such as child welfare agencies and departments of social services. Often, children need to leave their birth parents temporarily because of financial difficulties, abuse, alcoholism, or other serious problems. Foster children are often afraid, angry, or confused. They may have physical, **behavioral,** or mental problems. Foster parents need to have interest and enthusiasm, and provide a safe place and love and attention to the children in their care.

Safety, love, and attention are three important elements in the success of any family and certainly are necessary for the changing American family. The more we are **aware** of the many types of families in the United States, the better we can understand how to make each family a great place for a child to grow up in.

adjust	to get used to a place, to a thing, or to change
aware	knowing something
behavioral	related to the way a person acts
recognize	to know or identify from past experience of or knowledge
stepmother/stepfather	the wife/husband of one's father/mother and not one's natural parent
unite	to bring together to form a whole

Comprehension

▸EXERCISE 5 Write T (true) or F (false) for each statement. Then discuss your answers with a classmate.

__F__ 1. American families are basically all the same.

_____ 2. Many families in the United States today are blended families.

_____ 3. Blended families have stepmothers and stepfathers.

______ 4. Blended families are the easiest type of family to have.

______ 5. It is common now to see adoptive families with both birth children and adoptive children.

______ 6. An older adopted child brings memories and experiences into the adoptive family.

______ 7. Foster children leave their birth parents because of serious problems in the home.

______ 8. Foster homes are permanent homes during a crisis in a child's family life.

______ 9. Foster parents do not have to have any special qualities.

______ 10. Safety, love, and attention are important for families.

▸EXERCISE 6 List the positive and negative aspects of each type of family.

Blended Families

Advantages	Challenges
Members can learn from one another.	*Stepchildren do not automatically love their new siblings.*
	Stepchildren may not accept stepparents easily.

Adoptive Families

Advantages	Challenges

Foster Families

Advantages	Challenges

▸EXERCISE 7

A. Match the two parts of each sentence.

1. The number of blended families in the United States *h*
2. In blended families, children sometimes ______
3. Fairness and respect are ______
4. Some adoptive children come with a new ______
5. Adoptive parents who already have birth children ______
6. Foster parents need to have much interest and enthusiasm ______
7. Anger, confusion, and fear are ______
8. Money problems, abuse, and problems with alcohol ______
9. Foster parenting is temporary; adoption is ______
10. All children need to be safe, loved, and ______

a. paid attention to.
b. don't recognize or want a new parent.
c. are some of the reasons children go to foster homes.
d. permanent.
e. for the children in their care.
f. common among foster children.
g. language and culture.
h. is increasing.
i. required for a successful blended family.
j. can use their experience with their adopted children.

B. Now give examples to explain each word.

1. blended families *mother with two children, her second husband, his child from a previous marriage*
2. couple ______
3. foster mother ______
4. stepfather ______
5. challenge ______

▶**EXERCISE 8** **Read the questions and answer them orally with your teacher. Then answer them orally with a classmate. At home, write the answers for homework. Answer in complete sentences.**

About the Reading

1. What is the biggest difference today in American families? ____________________
____
2. What do children in blended families sometimes say to their stepfather or stepmother? ____________________
____
3. What is the challenge with teenagers in blended families? ____________________
____
4. In what ways does an adoptive child benefit from a family with birth children? ____
____
5. In what ways does an adoptive family benefit from an older adopted child? ________
____
6. What makes it difficult for a foster child to adjust to a foster family? __________
____
7. What three factors are important for the success of any family? ______________
____

What Do You Think?

8. What ideas do people in your country have about adopting or foster-parenting children? ____________________
____
9. Do you think you could be a foster parent? Why or why not? ________________
____
10. What other factors are important for a successful family? ________________
____

Vocabulary Practice

▸EXERCISE 9 Complete each sentence with a word from the box.

A.

siblings	challenge	~~couple~~	adopt	aware

1. Look at that ___couple___. You can see that they are very much in love.
2. Some people never have children of their own; they decide to ________________ one or more children.
3. Blending a family is a very big ________________, so you really have to work hard at it.
4. My two ________________ live in another city. I rarely get to see my brother and sister.
5. I am ________________ of the many resources for adoptive families; many other people know about these services too.

B.

stepmother	unite	adjust	birth children	behavioral

1. The children live with their father and his wife, their new ________________.
2. We need everyone in the family to work together; we have to ________________ ourselves.
3. Marc always has problems in school with other children. His counselor is helping him with his ________________ problems.
4. This is a big change, but we can ________________ to it.
5. They didn't adopt their children; they have two ________________.

▶EXERCISE 10

A. Draw a tic-tac-toe grid on a piece of paper like this:

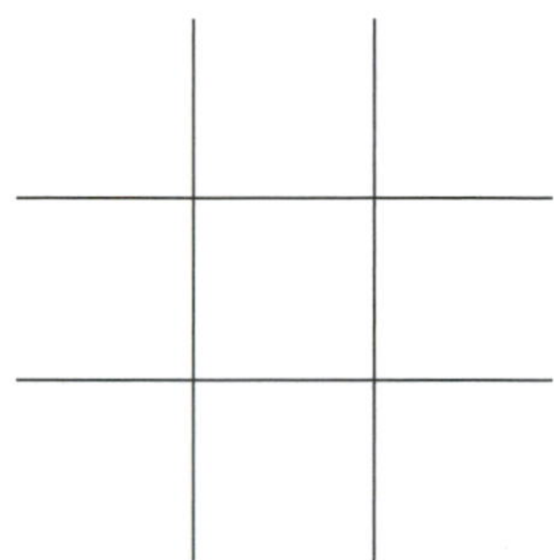

In each space, write one word from the vocabulary you learned so far in this chapter (nine words total). Then your teacher will read definitions of some of the words from the lesson. If you have written a word that matches the definition your teacher reads, mark it with an X. When you have three Xs in a row, horizontally, vertically, or diagonally, call out, "Tic-tac-toe, three in a row!"

B. Now guess these vocabulary words:

1. Cinderella had one of these ____________ and two of these ____________.
2. This word can also mean mixed ____________.
3. The same word completes these phrases: ____________ mother, ____________ children, ____________ day.

Reading 2 Family Challenges

Before You Read

▶EXERCISE 11 Write a phrase that means the same thing as each <u>underlined</u> word.

1. My baby is hungry; I need to <u>feed</u> her. ____________
2. That car is too expensive; it is not <u>affordable</u> for me. ____________
3. This classroom is too <u>crowded</u>! There isn't enough space. ____________

▸EXERCISE 12 Scan the reading to answer these questions.

1. What are four problems facing American families today? ______________________

____

2. What are two basic necessities that many American families have difficulty providing for their families? ______________________

____

3. What is one solution to the problem of time that many parents have in raising children? ______________________

____

Words from the Reading*

affordable	**feed**
crowded	**safe**

*Your teacher can help you understand these words and others listed at the end of the chapter and on the Web site at http://esl.college.hmco.com/students.

Read about special problems and solutions for modern families.

Family Challenges

Money, housing, education, and time—these are some necessities for raising a family. **Raising a family** is always difficult, but today's families in America face serious problems in meeting those needs. Finding solutions to those problems is necessary for the success of every family in the United States.

One significant problem is the financial difficulties that many families have. Even with two parents working, many Americans have a hard time feeding their families and providing them with other basic necessities, such as medical care. Financial difficulties cause a lot of stress for families. Sometimes families break up because of this stress. Various government programs and private organizations and individuals work hard to help families, but more solutions are needed.

Safe, affordable housing is another necessity for families, but many American families do not have good housing. Poor families spend a large percentage of their income on housing costs, and this leaves them little money for other things they need. Other families live in unsafe or crowded houses. Children require a roof over their heads, and many families **struggle** to provide this.

For the best chance at success in life, all children need a quality education. Everyone agrees on this, but people have different opinions about the best way to provide education for children. Not all schools are able to provide a quality education. The cost of a college education is **out of reach** for many families. Educators, families, and the general public need to find solutions for the educational success of all children.

With all of these needs, finding time to spend together is another challenge for parents and children. Parents are very creative in finding solutions to this. One mother writes a letter to her daughter during the day, writing one sentence each time she has a free moment. At the end of the day, she has a letter to give her child. Some working parents leave notes and little surprises for their children to find when they get home from school to an empty house. Many parents keep in contact with their children on their cell phones or by e-mail.

Parenting isn't easy—it never was. With the busy, challenging lives that we live in the United States today, raising a family is a **huge** responsibility. Parents, children, and community working together help make family life successful.

huge	of great size, extent, or quantity
out of reach	not possible
raising a family	taking care of or bringing up children
struggle	to make a hard effort

Comprehension

▸EXERCISE 13 Write T (true) or F (false) for each statement.

__T__ 1. American families face serious challenges in caring for their families.

_____ 2. Many American families have a hard time meeting their financial obligations.

_____ 3. Families with two parents working do not have worries about food or medical care.

_____ 4. Safe housing is not affordable for many American families.

_____ 5. A college education is affordable for all American families.

_____ 6. All American schools provide a quality education.

_____ 7. Parents don't have many solutions for the problem of time with their families.

_____ 8. Technology helps some parents keep in contact with their children.

_____ 9. Parenting is an easy job.

_____ 10. The community, parents, and families can work together to raise children.

▶EXERCISE 14 Complete the map of "Family Challenges" with the appropriate details.

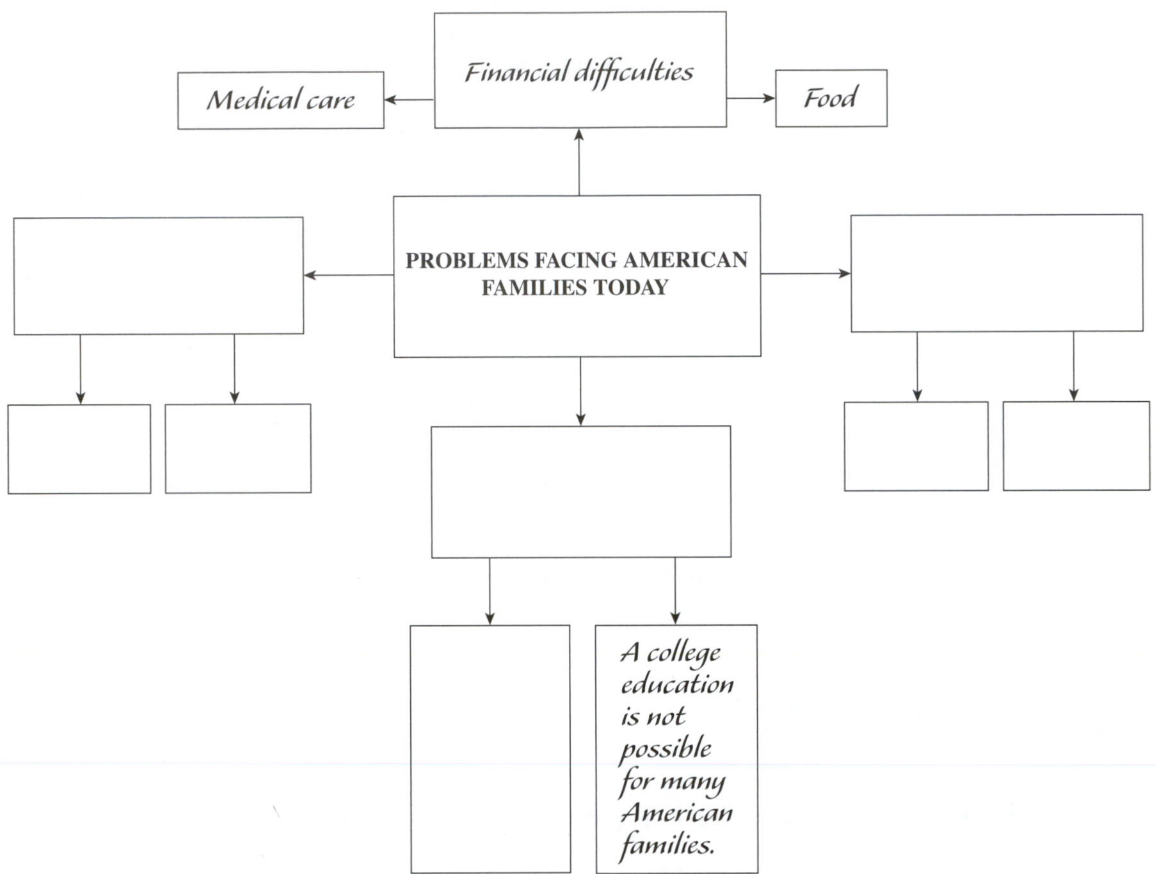

▶EXERCISE 15 Read the questions and answer them orally with your teacher. Then answer them orally with a classmate. At home, write the answers for homework. Answer in complete sentences.

About the Reading

1. What are some of the basic necessities for every family? ______________________

   ____

2. What is the problem with housing for families? ______________________

   ____

3. Who is responsible for providing a good education to children? ______

______

4. What is one mother's solution for finding time with her children? ______

______

5. What helps make family life successful? ______

______

What Do You Think?

6. What effect does a low-quality education have on a child? ______

______

7. What are some other solutions for the problem of time for families? ______

______

8. What problems do families face in your country? ______

______

Vocabulary Practice

▸EXERCISE 16 At home, write complete original sentences with the vocabulary words listed below. Then, in class, read your sentences to a partner with the word missing. Your partner should guess what the missing word is.

Example: My children are hungry. I need to ______ them. Your partner should guess "feed."

1. raise
2. struggle
3. affordable
4. crowded
5. safe
6. huge
7. out of reach
8. break up
9. roof
10. huge

Expansion Activities

▶ **Activity 1 Family Role Play** *In a group, write a dialogue for a blended family of four people, a husband and wife and their teenage daughters from different marriages. Include a problem they have and a solution to the problem. Then present the dialogue to the class.*

Example:

Daughter 1: I don't like my new stepsister. She always wears my clothes. I don't want her to live in this house!

Daughter 2: I don't like you either! You always listen to my phone conversations. Why don't you go live with your real father?

Father: We want you to be sisters. Why do we have so many problems?

Mother: This problem is very challenging.

Father: Isn't there another solution?

▶ **Activity 2 Letter to an Adoptive Child** *Write a letter from two parents who already have two birth children. The letter is to a child that they are going to adopt. Describe their family life to the adoptive child.*

To Our New Son/Daughter:

Welcome to the family! ____

____

____

____

____

____

____

____

____

____

Love,
Mom and Dad

Vocabulary List

Adjectives	Adverbs	Nouns		Verbs
adoptive	automatically	adoption	element	adjust
affordable	certainly	agency/agencies	enthusiasm	feed
aware	completely	birth child/ children	foster parent	provide
behavioral	especially	blended family/families	independence	raise a family
crowded	fairly	challenge	sibling	recognize
ethnic	legally	counselor	stepfamily/ stepfamilies	struggle
financial	rarely	couple	stepfather	unite
huge	temporarily	crisis	stepmother	
out of reach	usually			
safe				
temporary				

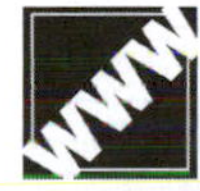

If you want to review vocabulary and complete additional activities related to this chapter, go to the *Read to Succeed 2* Web site at http://esl.college.hmco.com/students.

CHAPTER 4

Special People

Reading 1 Learning Disabilities and Technology

Before You Read

▸EXERCISE 1 Discuss these questions with a partner or a small group.

1. Are there disabled students at your school?
2. What examples can you give of a disability?
3. Can disabled students use a computer?

▶ **EXERCISE 2 Listen to your teacher read the sentences. Say the sentences after your teacher. Then match the sentences to the pictures. Write the correct letter next to the sentence.**

A.

B.

C.

D.

E.

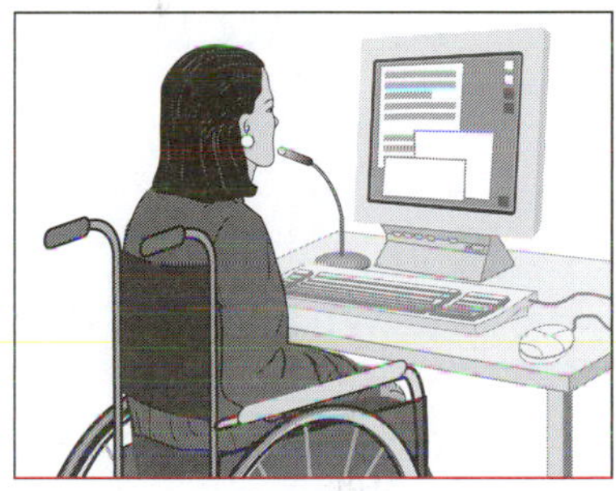

F.

1. Deaf students speak using sign language. ______
2. Many blind students attend college. ______
3. Physical accommodations such as ramps and larger doorways are important at schools. ______
4. Some schools offer students special accommodations in computer labs. ______
5. Blind students read using Braille. ______
6. There is assistive technology in computer labs for students with disabilities. ______

▸EXERCISE 3 Write the letter of the definition in the space next to the word.

1. deaf _____
2. disabled _____
3. blind _____

a. a person who can't see
b. a person who can't hear
c. a person who has a disability

Words from the Reading*

access	**accommodation**	**deaf**
blind	**disabled**	**disability**

*Your teacher can help you understand these words and others listed at the end of the chapter and on the Web site at http://esl.college.hmco.com/students.

▸EXERCISE 4 Scan the reading and answer these questions.

1. Who is attending schools more today? (paragraph 1) ______________________

____

2. What kind of disabilities are there? (paragraph 2) ______________________

____

3. What does assistive technology offer disabled students? (paragraph 3) __________

____

Read to find out about people with learning disabilities and the technology that helps them.

Learning Disabilities and Technology

More students with learning disabilities are attending schools today, and technology is helping them learn better. Almost fifty million people over five years old in the United States have some type of disability.* A disability is a mental or physical **impairment** that affects hearing, seeing, walking, working, or learning. An impairment is a health or learning problem. In the United States, students with disabilities in public schools from kindergarten through high school have access to education by law. Access means that these students have the right to receive an education at a public school. The

*U.S. Census, 2000.

law also requires colleges that receive money from the federal government to provide help for these students. Schools and colleges must offer disabled students accommodations to help them learn. Examples of accommodations are more time to take a test, ramps for wheelchairs, sign language interpreters, and computers that speak.

Some types of physical or **psychological** disabilities make it especially difficult for students to learn. Some students have **chronic** physical health problems that make it painful to go to classes. Others have attention deficit disorder (ADD), so they are less **attentive** and can be **hyperactive.** Other people are blind or have low vision. Some students are deaf or have a hearing loss. Another type of learning disability is caused by a **neurological** problem. A blow to the head or a disease can result in neurological problems. Some students can't move parts of their body because of illness or accident, or because they were born that way. Finally, some people have a psychological disability that makes class attendance more difficult because they are depressed at times. Learning is harder and more limited for all these students, but there is help from technology.

Assistive technology offers immediate learning help for disabled students. This technology assists students with learning disabilities to be more independent. The type of assistive technology depends on the student's disability. The good news for students and schools is that assistive technology is now easier to use and cheaper to buy. If students can't write or can't use their hands, they can use a microphone and a special computer that types what the students say. For blind students, a computer with assistive technology can read words on a computer screen so students hear the words. Other special computers can read a book aloud for students to hear.

Assistive technology makes learning more accessible for disabled students and gives them confidence. It makes education more possible for these students.

assistive	helpful or supportive
attentive	paying attention to or looking at closely
chronic	very serious and permanent
hyperactive	more active than normal
impairment	a damage or lessening of quality
neurological	having to do with the nervous system
psychological	mental

Comprehension

▶EXERCISE 5 Write T (true) or F (false) for each statement. Then discuss your answers with a classmate.

_____ 1. Disabled students do not attend schools in the United States.

_____ 2. *Access* means the right to get an education.

_____ 3. No colleges in the United States provide help to disabled students.

_____ 4. An accommodation is similar to a recommendation.

_____ 5. Disabilities can be physical or psychological.

_____ 6. *ADD* in this reading means the opposite of *subtract*.

_____ 7. A depressed person is never absent from class.

_____ 8. Assistive technology is becoming easier to use and cheaper to buy.

_____ 9. Education is more difficult with assistive technology.

_____ 10. Assistive technology makes students more dependent.

▶EXERCISE 6 Circle the letter of the main idea for each paragraph.

Paragraph 1:

a. Assistive technology helps many years later.

b. There are different kinds of disabilities.

c. Disabled students are going to school more, and technology is helping them.

Paragraph 2:

a. Physically disabled people learn more easily than students with psychological disabilities.

b. It is more difficult to learn with disabilities.

c. People who are deaf have a physical disability.

Paragraph 3:

a. Assistive technology gives disabled students help with learning.

b. Assistive technology is now more expensive but easier to use.

c. Assistive technology offers assistance only to blind students.

▶EXERCISE 7 Circle the letter of the correct answer.

1. What is a disability?
   a. an impairment that is temporary
   b. a mental or physical impairment
   c. a physical impairment
2. What does access to education mean in the United States?
   a. Disabled students have the right to get an education at a public school.
   b. Students with disabilities can attend only a few schools.
   c. Disabled students have the freedom to get an education at a private school.
3. Colleges that receive money from the federal government
   a. have larger programs for students with disabilities.
   b. have more money for all programs.
   c. must provide assistance to students with learning disabilities.
4. Offering a disabled student more time to take a test is an example of
   a. an access.
   b. an assistive.
   c. an accommodation.
5. Learning disabilities make it ______ for students to learn.
   a. more serious
   b. harder
   c. more independent
6. What can make it physically painful for a student to go to classes?
   a. a psychological disability
   b. a neurological problem
   c. a chronic physical health problem
7. People who don't pay attention and are very active may have ______
   a. ADD.
   b. a hearing problem.
   c. a vision problem.
8. What causes a learning disability?
   a. not having an education
   b. a neurological problem
   c. an illness

▶**EXERCISE 8 Answer the questions orally with your teacher. Then answer the questions orally with a classmate. At home, write the answers for homework. Answer in complete sentences.**

1. What is assistive technology? *Assistive technology uses computers to help disabled students learn.*
2. What does assistive technology offer disabled students? ______
3. Do disabled students become more independent or less independent with assistive technology? ______
4. What is a disability? ______
5. Is assistive technology now more difficult for students to use? ______
6. What can the computer do for students who can't write? ______
7. How can blind students know what is on a computer screen? ______
8. Why is assistive technology good for students with learning disabilities? ______
9. Why do some colleges have to help students with disabilities? ______
10. Why are accommodations in schools important for disabled students? ______

Vocabulary Practice

▸EXERCISE 9 Complete the paragraph with words from the box.

right	disabilities	technology	impairment	attentive	independent
disabled	confidence	Braille	blind	microphone	difficult

David is attending a college in his town. There are many students with physical and psychological ________________ at his college. He is in the ________________ student program at his college, and he attends school with his seeing-eye dog, Rusty. David has a serious eye ________________. He is completely ________________ and cannot see. He must read books in ________________ or listen to them on the computer. He feels very fortunate because he has the ________________ to a college education. When he is in class, he is very ________________ and pays attention to everything his teachers say. He uses assistive ________________ in the computer lab to write his papers. He uses a ________________ to speak to the computer; then the computer types his papers. He is succeeding in college, and this is giving him more ________________. Thanks to assistive technology, David is becoming more ________________, and learning is now less ________________.

►EXERCISE 10 Write the correct antonym from "Learning Disabilities and Technology" for the underlined word or words. An antonym is a word with the opposite meaning.

Paragraph 1:

1. His ability to learn is getting worse. ____________________
2. He gets less time on tests. ____________________
3. He is attending a private school. ____________________

Paragraph 2:

4. Learning is easier for some students. ____________________
5. I am more attentive in class than you. ____________________
6. She has perfect vision. ____________________
7. We have good hearing. ____________________

Paragraph 3:

8. Some assistive technology is more expensive than others. ____________________
9. A two-year-old child is very dependent. ____________________
10. My tests are harder on the computer. ____________________

GRAMMAR

Grammar Hints: Review of Present Progressive

Present progressive tense

to be + verb + *-ing*

I am learning more about technology. (learn)

We are taking a test now. (take)

Note: For verbs that end in e, drop the e before adding *-ing*.

►EXERCISE 11 Complete each sentence with the present progressive form of the verb in parentheses.

1. She ______ ____________ a large university this school year. (attend)
2. Assistive technology ______ ____________ disabled students now. (help)
3. Colleges ______ ____________ accommodations for students with disabilities. (offer)

4. My college ______ ____________ mc with assistive technology. (provide)
5. My friends and I ______ ____________ special computers for blind students. (use—drop final *e*)
6. I ______ ____________ all my books on a computer this year. (read)
7. I ______ ____________ all my homework on time this semester. (complete—drop final *e*)
8. She ______ ____________ her counselor in five minutes. (meet)
9. Disabled students ______ ____________ in school thanks to technology. (succeed)
10. My classmates and I ______ ____________ an important test in five minutes. (take—drop final *e*)

Reading 2 Assistive Technology

Before You Read

▶EXERCISE 12 Write a synonym for each underlined word. Choose from "Words from the Reading."

1. My teachers permit more time on tests for me. ____________________
2. Walking around school is problematic at times. ____________________
3. He has a mechanical wheelchair. ____________________

▶EXERCISE 13 Scan the reading to answer these questions.

1. What are the students using for their classes? ____________________

____

2. What program is Vasyl in? ____________________

____

3. How is Oscar's vision? ____________________

____

Words from the Reading*

allow	**motorized**	**software**
speech	**troublesome**	

*Your teacher can help you understand these words and others listed at the end of the chapter and on the Web site at http://esl.college.hmco.com/students.

Read to find out how technology helps people with learning disabilities.

Assistive Technology

Vasyl and Oscar are students with physical disabilities who are using technology to make their classes less difficult. Their college knows that students with disabilities find classes more troublesome than most students do, so the college provides assistive technology to make classes more enjoyable. Newer technology is assisting Oscar and Vasyl in reading, writing, note taking, spelling, and hearing. The college they are attending and their teachers allow or make accommodations for them. They are using technology with special **hardware** and **software** programs, and their teachers are permitting more time for tests.

Vasyl is using technology in his computer support specialist program because he doesn't have the use of his hands or feet. He uses a motorized wheelchair to move around campus. The college has elevators and special ramps for students like Vasyl who can't use stairs. Vasyl has good vision and speaks well, but he can't write with a pen or a computer, take notes in class, or write papers in the same way other students do. The college is providing Vasyl with another student who is a **note taker** in class. Vasyl uses a computer with **voice recognition** software to write his papers and check his spelling. He speaks into a microphone; then the computer changes his speech to words on the screen that he can see. If there is a mistake on the screen, Vasyl can ask the computer to change the mistake with his voice. He can also give the spell checker voice commands.

Oscar has very low vision, so he can't see the board in class, read a book, or see a regular computer screen. It takes him longer to write his papers than it takes other students, and his eyes become more fatigued. He is taking classes in the English as a Second Language program. Not only is he learning English, but he is also learning new technology that is assisting him with English. In class, he uses a television screen and a **telephoto lens** to see the board or his book. He also has a note taker in class. To write his papers outside of class, he uses a computer with a larger letter keyboard with a **magnifying glass.** He can look through the magnifying glass and see the keyboard or the computer screen. His computer also uses a talking **word processor** that repeats what he writes. He enjoys reading more now because a computer **scans** his books, changes the text into speech, and reads it aloud to him. His blind friends also read books in this way if they are not using Braille books.

Studying in college is more difficult for Vasyl and Oscar because of their disabilities, but they are happy with the new technology. Both students are succeeding with assistive technology.

hardware	computers, screens, keyboards
magnifying glass	a lens that makes small things look big
note taker	a person who takes notes for another person
scan	to look through quickly
software	computer programs on CDs or a computer's hard drive
telephoto lens	a lens that brings far objects near
voice recognition	a computer program that recognizes a voice
word processor	a computer that produces words

Comprehension

▶EXERCISE 14 Write T (true) or F (false) for each statement.

_____ 1. Vasyl walks around school and can use stairs.

_____ 2. Oscar can see the classroom board a little.

_____ 3. Vasyl needs to use a telephoto lens to see the computer screen.

_____ 4. Oscar is studying English as a Second Language.

_____ 5. The two students have disabilities that are the same.

_____ 6. Oscar takes notes for Vasyl in class.

_____ 7. The college they are attending offers accommodations for them.

_____ 8. Vasyl wants to be a computer science teacher.

_____ 9. Oscar is a blind student.

_____ 10. Both students use a computer with a larger keyboard.

▶EXERCISE 15 Circle the letter of the correct answer.

1. Assistive technology is making Oscar and Vasyl's classes ______.
   a. harder b. less difficult c. less technical
2. Students with disabilities find regular classes ______.
   a. easier b. less difficult c. more problematic
3. The college they are attending is permitting ______.
   a. accommodations b. wheelchairs c. special books
4. Vasyl is in the ______ program.
   a. ESL b. computer science c. computer support specialist
5. What does Vasyl use to get around campus?
   a. a regular wheelchair b. a seeing-eye dog c. a motorized wheelchair
6. What disability does Oscar have?
   a. a hearing loss b. low vision c. blindness
7. Oscar's eyes become ______ when he writes a long paper.
   a. blind b. tired c. stressful
8. A computer with voice recognition software recognizes the students' ______.
   a. speech b. hearing c. writing
9. What does a note taker do for the students in class?
   a. types notes b. takes notes c. writes papers
10. What is software used with?
   a. wheelchairs b. keyboards c. hardware

▶EXERCISE 16 Circle the letter of the main idea for each paragraph.

Paragraph 1:

a. Assistive technology is helping Vasyl and Oscar.
b. Teachers are permitting more time for tests.
c. Vasyl and Oscar are disabled students.

Paragraph 2:

a. Technology is helping nondisabled students in their majors.
b. Vasyl uses a motorized wheelchair.
c. Vasyl is disabled, so he is using technology to study for his major.

Paragraph 3:

a. Oscar is studying English to be a computer support specialist.

b. Oscar can't use his hands, feet, or eyes, so he uses technology.

c. Because of Oscar's poor vision, he uses a variety of technology to help him in his classes.

Vocabulary Practice

▶EXERCISE 17 Complete each sentence with a word or phrase from the box.

motorized	scan	hardware	software	word processor
allows	speech	troublesome	board	magnifying glass

1. A talking ____________ on the computer repeats what Oscar writes.
2. Vasyl's wheelchair is ____________.
3. The students' college ____________ accommodations for disabled students.
4. Oscar can see the ____________ with a telephoto lens.
5. Special computers ____________ books for blind people.
6. Some computers that scan a book change it to ____________ for students.
7. Oscar and Vasyl use special voice recognition ____________ on the computer.
8. Oscar can see the larger keyboard by using a ____________.
9. Computers, keyboards, and scanners are ____________.
10. If disabled students do not have assistive technology, classes are ____________.

▸EXERCISE 18 Complete the sentences with the comparative form of the word in parentheses.

With regular short adjectives of one or two syllables, add *-r* or *-er*.

1. Vasyl and Oscar need a ___longer___ time for tests. (long)
2. Classes are ________________ for disabled students. (hard)
3. Technology is ________________ than before. (cheap)
4. ________________ assistive technology is now available. (new)
5. Oscar uses a ________________ keyboard. (large)

With adjectives that end in *y*, change *y* to *i* and add *-er*.

6. Some students are ___busier___ than others. (busy)
7. Learning is ________________ with assistive technology. (easy)
8. Students arrive ________________ to school if they take the bus. (early)
9. The cafeteria will be ________________ after lunch. (dirty)
10. If students get more rest, they are ________________. (healthy)

With long adjectives, write *more* or *less* before the adjective.

11. In the past, technology was ___more expensive___ (expensive)
12. Learning is ________________ for disabled students with assistive technology. (difficult)
13. Students with ADD are ________________ in class. (attentive)
14. Disabled students are becoming ________________ with technology. (independent)
15. Classes are now ________________ than before for Oscar and Vasyl. (enjoyable)

▸EXERCISE 19 Read the questions and answer them orally with your teacher. Then answer the questions orally with a classmate. At home, write the answers for homework. Use complete sentences.

Paragraph 1:

1. What do Vasyl and Oscar have? ____

____

2. What is technology assisting Oscar and Vasyl with? ______________________________

3. What is their college allowing, or making, for them this year? ______________________________

Paragraph 2:

4. What disability does Vasyl have? ______________________________

5. How does Vasyl climb stairs? ______________________________

6. What is the college providing him with? ______________________________

7. How does Vasyl write papers for his classes? ______________________________

Paragraph 3:

8. What does Oscar take longer to do? ______________________________

9. What two things is he learning? ______________________________

10. Why does he use a magnifying glass? ______________________________

What Do You Think?

11. Do you think giving disabled students more time for a test is fair? Why or why not?

____

12. Do you think learning disability programs in college are fair? Why or why not?

____

Expansion Activities

► **Activity 1 Answer Questions About Statistics** *Look at the statistics for disabled Americans; then answer the questions in complete sentences.*

Disabilities in the United States for Ages 16–64*

Total U.S. Population, 16–64	178,687,234
Total disabled, 16–64	33,153,211

Type of Disability	Number (Percentage)
Employment	21,287,570 (11.9%)
Physical	11,150,365 (6.2%)
Mental	6,764,439 (3.8%)
Sensory	4,123,902 (2.3%)

*U.S. Census, 2000.

1. Where do the statistics come from? ____________________
2. What was the total U.S. population 16–64 years old in 2000? ____________________
3. How many people 16–64 years of age were disabled in 2000? ____________________
4. What type of disability was there the most of? ____________________
5. How many people were physically disabled? ____________________
6. What are some examples of employment disabilities? ____________________
7. Why do you think so many people were employment disabled? ____________________
8. What are some examples of sensory disabilities? ____________________

   ____
9. What do you think are the disability statistics for people over 64? ____________________

   ____
10. What disabilities have you seen? ____________________

    ____

▶ Activity 2 Crossword Puzzle *Complete the puzzle using the clues provided.*

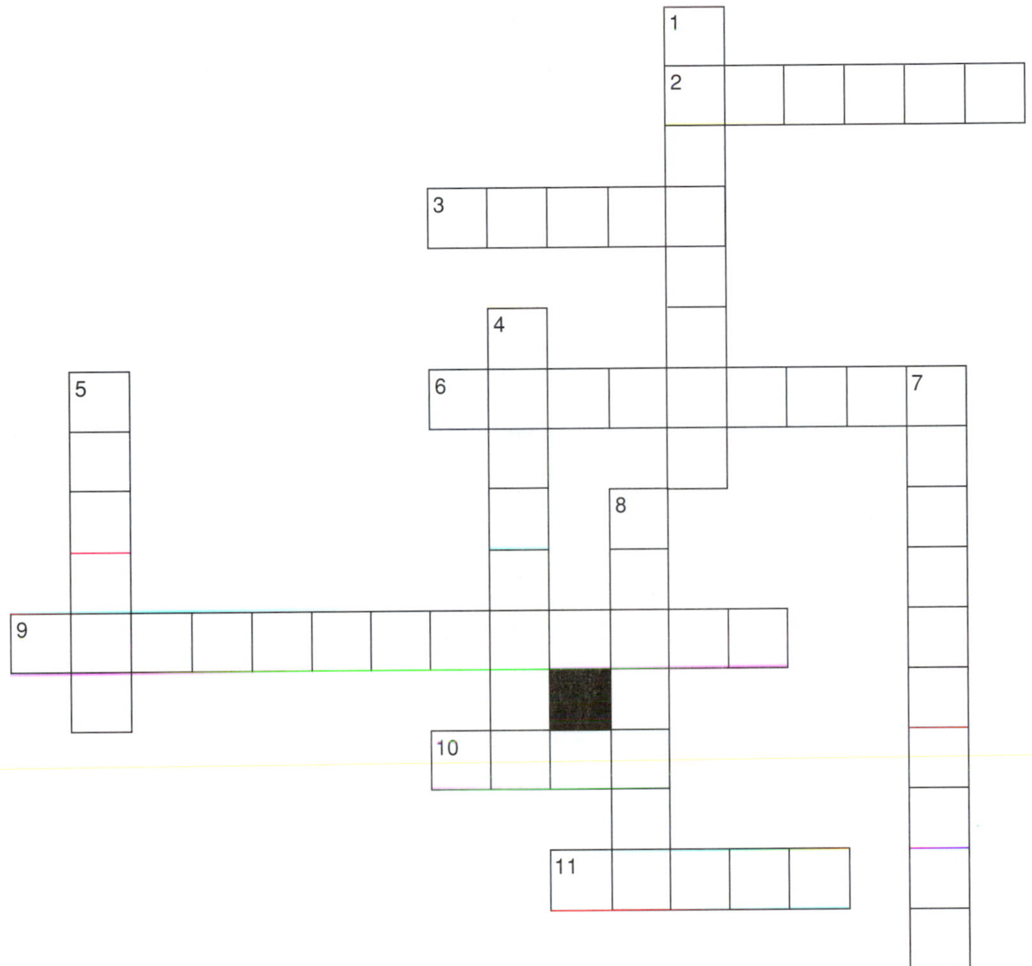

Across

2. right to an education
3. unable to see
6. a synonym for *mechanical*
9. more time on a test or ramps
10. unable to hear
11. a synonym for *permit*

Down

1. computers, screens, and keyboards
4. programs for computers for students
5. talking
7. a physical or mental impairment
8. something that hurts

Vocabulary List

Adjectives

assistive
attentive
chronic
difficult
disabled
enjoyable
fair
independent
learning
low
mechanical
mental
motorized
neurological
painful
physical
psychological
troublesome

Adverbs

easily

Nouns

access
accommodation
board
Braille
confidence
disability/disabilities
education
hardware
impairment
interpreter
magnifying glass
microphone
note taker
note taking
ramp
right
screen
sign language
software
speech
spelling
technology
telephoto lens
vision
voice recognition
wheelchair
word processor

Abilities

hearing
learning
seeing
speaking
walking

Body

eye
foot
hand
head
voice

Disabilities

attention deficit disorder
blind
chronic physical health problem
deaf
hearing loss
hyperactive
low vision
neurological problem
physical disability
psychological disability

Verbs

affect
allow
assist
attend
become
learn
mean
offer
permit
require
scan

If you want to review vocabulary and complete additional activities related to this chapter, go to the *Read to Succeed 2* Web site at http://esl.college.hmco.com/students.

UNIT 2 Readings in the Social Sciences

CHAPTER 5
The First Americans

Reading 1 The First Americans

Before You Read

▸EXERCISE 1 Discuss these questions with a partner or a small group.

1. What people are Americans?
2. What country did you come from?
3. Why do many immigrants come to the United States?

▸EXERCISE 2 Look at the pictures and write the correct letter next to the definition.

A. tepee

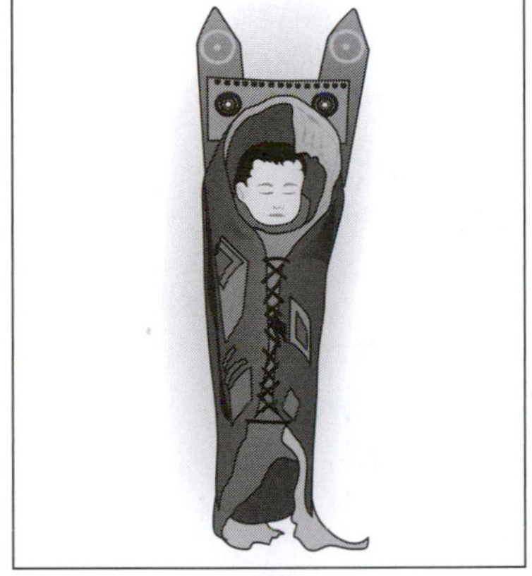

B. papoose

C. totem pole

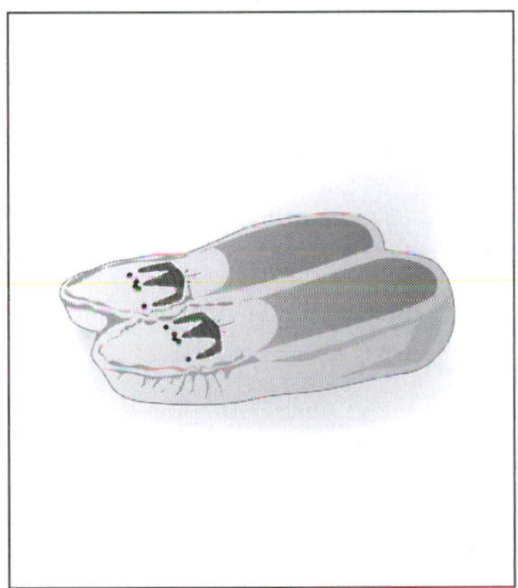

D. moccasins

E. headdress

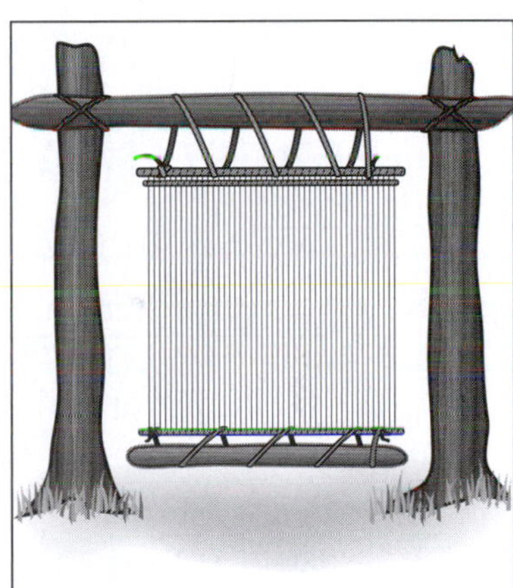

F. loom

1. An American Indian house made of animal skin. _____
2. One type of American Indian shoe. _____
3. What some important American Indians put on their head. _____
4. The word for *baby* for some American Indians. _____
5. A beautiful wooden monument or artifact from Native Americans of the Pacific Northwest. _____
6. Tool for making blankets and rugs. _____

▶EXERCISE 3 Scan the reading and write the synonym.

1. to move from one place to another ________________ (paragraph 1)
2. a large group of Native Americans ________________ (paragraph 2)
3. American Indians ________________ (paragraph 3)

Words from the Reading*

the Americas	**migrate**
Asia	**Native American**
Bering Strait	**reservation**
civilization	**tribe**
European	

*Your teacher can help you understand these words and others listed at the end of the chapter and on the Web site at http://esl.college.hmco.com/students.

▶EXERCISE 4 Scan the reading and answer these questions.

1. What is the title of the reading? ________________

____

2. What do you think the reading is about? ________________

____

3. Who were the first Americans? ________________

____

4. What is one thing that Native Americans introduced to Europeans? ________________

____

5. What is one Native American word in the English language? ________________

____

Read to find out about the first Americans.*

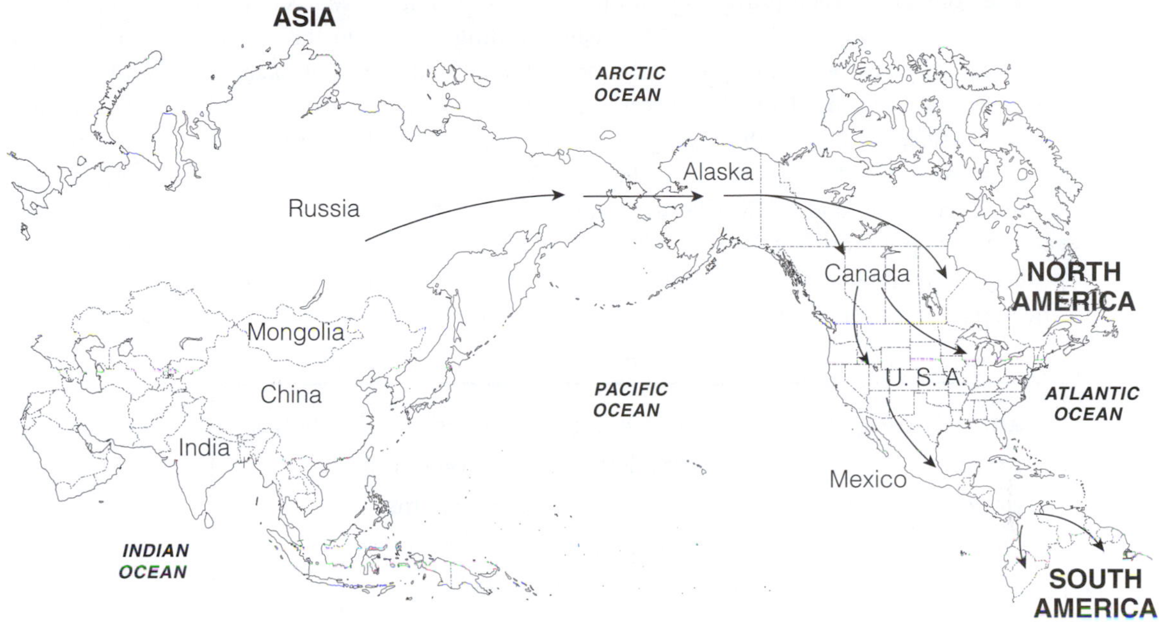

Migration of Native Americans to the Americas

The First Americans

The first people in the Americas were the Native Americans, or American Indians. They walked from Asia to Alaska and arrived in the Americas 40,000 to 100,000 years ago. **Anthropologists** don't know exactly when they arrived, but there are Native American sites and **artifacts** thousands of years old in the Americas. The Indians slowly migrated from the Bering Strait and settled throughout the Americas as far south as the southern **tip** of South America. The migration lasted thousands of years.

Native Americans developed advanced civilizations in Chile, Peru, Bolivia, Guatemala, Mexico, the United States, and Canada. They studied nature, astronomy, and mathematics. The Mayans in Mexico were one of the first people to use the number zero, and they had a very accurate calendar. The Mayans also built one of the first observatories to study the planets, stars, and planting seasons. These Indians built pyramids, mounds, and elaborate temples in different parts of the Americas. Art, music, books (codices), storytelling, astronomy, and musical instruments were important to them. When the Europeans came to the Americas, Indians introduced them to many foods, such as beans, corn, potatoes, tomatoes, chocolate, and avocados. The Indians in the United States lived in organized societies and used different languages. They formed political groups, or tribes, to have power. They gathered in **peace councils** to talk about serious problems with unfriendly tribes.

Native American and European cultures met and sometimes blended in the Americas. We still use many Native American words in English, such as *brave* for young soldier, *igloo* for an ice house, *tepee* for an animal-skin house, *moccasins* for shoes, *pow-wow* for a meeting, and *papoose* for baby. The Wampanoag Indians helped the first Europeans, the Pilgrims, during their first year in the Americas. The

*Related classes to take or visit: Native American studies, U.S. history.

Pilgrims had a special meal to thank the Wampanoags. Americans celebrate Thanksgiving today to remember this special friendship and meal.

The contact between Europeans and Indians has also had a very sad and violent history. When the first Europeans came in the 1500s, they began killing American Indians and stealing their land. The American Indians fought many battles to protect their land from Europeans who wanted it. After many Europeans arrived, the United States moved American Indians from their lands to reservations. The "Trail of Tears" refers to the U.S. government's move of the Cherokees in 1838 from their land in Georgia, when gold was discovered there, to Oklahoma. The Cherokees had to walk 1,000 miles in winter conditions, and 4,000 Cherokees died. Today, American Indians on reservations suffer from economic depression and lack of educational opportunities. It is difficult for them to escape from poverty. Some people think the United States owes Native Americans money for the **theft** of their land. The early contact between Europeans and Native Americans has an effect even today.

anthropologist	a scientist who studies people and societies
artifact	a thing made and used a long time ago
peace council	a group that discusses problems
theft	the crime of stealing something
tip	the end or point of something

Comprehension

▸EXERCISE 5 Write T (true) or F (false) for each statement.

_____ 1. The first people in the Americas were Europeans.

_____ 2. *Native American* is the same as *American Indian*.

_____ 3. The Native Americans probably migrated from Africa.

_____ 4. They arrived in the Americas 6,000–10,000 years ago.

_____ 5. The Indians slowly migrated south.

_____ 6. A large group of Native Americans together for power is called a peace council.

_____ 7. The Mayans did not use mathematics.

_____ 8. The U.S. government moved many Indians to reservations.

_____ 9. Native American and European contact had a happy ending.

_____ 10. American Indian educational opportunities are very good.

▶EXERCISE 6 Circle the letter of the correct answer.

1. What direction did the Native Americans migrate?
   a. north b. south c. west
2. What did Native Americans start in many parts of the Americas?
   a. Thanksgiving b. advanced civilizations c. tepees
3. What is a large group of Native Americans called?
   a. moccasins b. a tribe c. a migration
4. What did peace councils talk about?
   a. reservations b. civilizations c. serious problems
5. What is the name for a small ice house?
   a. igloo b. moccasins c. brave
6. Where did the United States move many Native Americans?
   a. Europe b. reservations c. societies
7. Who did the Wampanoag help in the new land?
   a. Europeans b. Indians c. soldiers
8. What Indian group walked the "Trail of Tears"?
   a. Hopi b. Cherokee c. Wampanoag

▶EXERCISE 7 Complete the sentence with the main idea for each paragraph.

Paragraph 1: Native Americans migrated *throughout the Americas.*

Paragraph 2: Many Native American societies were ____________________.

Paragraph 3: Native Americans and Europeans ____________________.

Paragraph 4: The history of Indians and Europeans ____________________.

►**EXERCISE 8** **Answer the questions orally with your teacher. Then answer the questions orally with a classmate. At home, write the answers for homework. Answer in complete sentences.**

About the Reading

1. Where did the first Americans walk from? ______________________________

   ____

2. When did they arrive? ______________________________

   ____

3. Where did they migrate to? ______________________________

   ____

4. What did they start in the Americas? ______________________________

   ____

5. What was the "Trail of Tears"? ______________________________

   ____

6. What is a tribe? ______________________________

   ____

7. Where did the United States move the Cherokees? ______________________________

   ____

8. Why do we celebrate Thanksgiving? ______________________________

   ____

***Why* Questions Ask for a Reason or Opinion.**

9. Why do you think the Indians walked to South America from Alaska? *The Indians walked to South America to look for food and better weather.*

10. Why do you think the Europeans wanted the Native Americans' land? ______________

    ____

11. Why do many Native Americans live on reservations today? ______________________

____

12. Do you think the U.S. government owes the American Indians money for their land? Why or why not? ______________________________

____

Vocabulary Practice

▸EXERCISE 9

A. Read the whole paragraph first. Then complete the paragraph with words from the box.

Americas	tribes	Asia	civilizations	Europeans
migrated	councils	slowly	Native Americans	reservations

The first people in the Americas were the ______________. They walked from ______________ and arrived in the Americas thousands of years ago. They ______________ south little by little, migrating ______________ from Alaska to South America. In many parts of the ______________ they started advanced ______________. They lived in large, organized groups called ______________. The Native Americans formed peace ______________ to talk about problems. When many ______________ arrived in the United States from Europe, the U.S. government moved many Native Americans to ______________.

B. Use these words in a sentence.

1. last ______________________________
2. settle ______________________________
3. elaborate ______________________________
4. peace ______________________________
5. nature ______________________________

▶EXERCISE 10 Match the word with the definition.

1. brave ______
2. migrate ______
3. moccasins ______
4. Native Americans ______
5. papoose ______
6. tribe ______
7. tepee ______
8. Asia ______
9. reservations ______
10. Thanksgiving ______

a. celebration where Native Americans thanked Europeans
b. a large group of Native Americans
c. a Native American soldier
d. an animal-skin house
e. to move from one place to another
f. animal-skin shoes
g. where the U.S. government moved the Native Americans
h. the first Americans
i. a Native American baby
j. where the Native Americans were from

Reading 2 Immigrants in the United States

Before You Read

▶EXERCISE 11 Discuss these questions with a partner or small group.

1. Where is the Statue of Liberty?
2. When is Independence Day in your native country or in the United States?
3. What are some American symbols (signs that represent something)?
4. When did Europeans first come to the Americas?
5. Why did you come to the United States?
6. How is the United States of today different from or the same as the United States of the 1700s?

►EXERCISE 12 Listen to your teacher read the sentences. Say the sentences after your teacher. Then match the sentences to the pictures. Write the correct letter next to the sentence.

A.

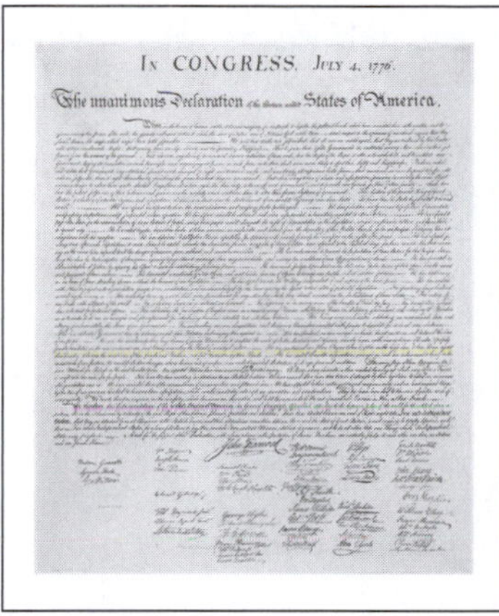

IN CONGRESS, JULY 4, 1776.

The unanimous Declaration of the [illegible] States of America.

B.

C.

D.

E.

F.

_____ 1. The Statue of Liberty in New York is a symbol of freedom for many European immigrants.

_____ 2. The thirteen colonies celebrated the Declaration of Independence on July 4, 1776.

_____ 3. The bald eagle is a symbol of the U.S. government.

_____ 4. After 1892, European immigrants arrived by ship at Ellis Island, New York.

_____ 5. The first European immigrants arrived in Jamestown, Virginia, in 1607.

_____ 6. The Liberty Bell is a symbol of U.S. independence.

▶EXERCISE 13 Write T (true) or F (false) for each statement.

______ 1. People use cotton to make clothes.

______ 2. Chains are usually made from metal.

______ 3. Factories are places where people always work outside.

Words from the Reading*

chain	**factory**
colony	**flag**
cotton	**Jamestown**

*Your teacher can help you understand these words and others listed at the end of the chapter and on the Web site at http://esl.college.hmco.com/students.

▶EXERCISE 14 Work with a partner to scan the reading and answer the questions.

1. What is the title of the reading?
2. What is an immigrant?
3. What do you predict the reading is about?

Read to learn about immigrants to the United States.*

Immigrants in the United States

The United States is a country of **immigrants.** After the Native Americans, all people here have an immigrant past except African slaves and their **descendants.** The first immigrants were Europeans, and they arrived in Jamestown, Virginia, in 1607. They arrived from England on a **ship** named the *Mayflower* to escape religious **persecution.** After these first immigrants, many other groups of immigrants continued to arrive. By 1619, African **slaves** also started to arrive in Jamestown. They came in chains on slave ships. Many Africans died on the ships during the long trip. The slaves were separated from their families and sold to Europeans in the United States. The Europeans bought the African slaves to work on their cotton and tobacco **plantations,** or very large farms.

*Related classes to take or visit: U.S. history, ethnic studies.

The first European immigrants formed thirteen colonies under England. The thirteen colonies were not happy with the mother country, England. The colonies were paying taxes but did not have power. They decided to fight and won their independence. The new Americans wrote the Declaration of Independence. It said that all men were created equal, but it did not include Indians, African slaves, or women. The colonies celebrated their Declaration of Independence from England on July 4, 1776. They became a new country, and George Washington was the first president. The colonies later became the first states. The first U.S. flag had thirteen stars and stripes. The first U.S. census to count the population started in 1790.

In the 1700s, 1800s, and 1900s, many immigrants came to the United States from different countries. Everyone wanted jobs, freedom, an education, and better opportunities. The Germans, English, Scottish, and Irish came in the 1700s. In the early 1800s, the European immigrants were better educated and had money. From 1850 to 1920, many of the Europeans who came were poor and were from Ireland, Russia, Poland, Hungary, and southern Europe. Like all immigrants, they also wanted jobs, opportunities, and a good future.

From the 1950s to 2003, many new immigrants came because of war, or for economic or political reasons. Many of these people were Asian or Hispanic. From 1942 to 2003, many immigrant workers arrived without legal documents to work in American homes, factories, restaurants, hotels, and other businesses. Many of them work in agriculture—one of the most difficult jobs. The U.S. Census says that between 1971 and 1975, about 385,000 legal immigrants also arrived each year. Some people think that these new immigrants contribute to the U.S. economy and help keep prices down. Some Americans think that the United States needs the immigrants' energy and positive attitude about working in low-level or difficult jobs. Other people disagree with this idea and think these immigrants take the jobs that Americans need or want.

descendant	a person who comes after others in the same bloodline
immigrant	a person who leaves one country to live in another
persecution	bad treatment or harsh control
plantation	a large farm where slaves worked
ship	a large boat
slave	a human being who is bought and sold

Comprehension

▸EXERCISE 15 Write T (true) or F (false) for each statement.

______ 1. African slaves arrived in Jamestown, Virginia, in 1607.

______ 2. The first European immigrants arrived on a ship, the *Mayflower.*

______ 3. There were no black slaves in the thirteen colonies.

______ 4. The thirteen colonies were under the rule of England.

______ 5. The colonies wanted independence from England.

______ 6. The Declaration of Independence was signed on July 14, 1789.

______ 7. Abraham Lincoln was the first president.

______ 8. There were fifty stars and stripes on the first U.S. flag.

______ 9. The new immigrants do not want to work.

______ 10. The newest immigrants now are from Europe and Africa.

▸EXERCISE 16 Complete the sentence with the main idea for each paragraph.

Paragraph 1: The United States is a country ______________________________

____.

Paragraph 2: The thirteen colonies wanted ______________________________

____.

Paragraph 3: In the 1700s, 1800s, and 1900s, ______________________________

____.

Paragraph 4: Immigrants continue to arrive and ______________________________

____.

▸EXERCISE 17

A. Match the two parts of each sentence.

1. The United States is ______.
2. All people in the United States who are not Native Americans or descendants of slaves ______.
3. The first European immigrants ______.
4. The first African slaves arrived ______.
5. There were thirteen ______.
6. The Declaration of Independence ______.
7. The thirteen colonies wanted ______.
8. The first president was ______.
9. There were thirteen stripes and thirteen ______.
10. Many of the new immigrants are ______.

a. Asian or Hispanic
b. stars on the first U.S. flag
c. George Washington
d. a country of immigrants
e. colonies under England
f. have an immigrant past
g. arrived in Jamestown in 1607
h. in Jamestown in 1619
i. was signed on July 4, 1776
j. independence from England

B. Write some notes about when, why, where, how, and with whom you came to the United States.

1. When? ________________________________

____

2. Why? ________________________________

____

3. Where? ________________________________

____

4. How? ________________________________

____

5. With whom? ________________________________

____

▸EXERCISE 18 Answer the questions orally with your teacher. Then answer the questions orally with a classmate. At home, write the answers for homework. Answer in complete sentences.

About the Reading

1. Who has an immigrant past in the United States? ______

2. When did the first European immigrants arrive? ______

3. How did they come? ______

4. When did black slaves arrive in the United States? ______

5. When was the Declaration of Independence signed? ______

6. What did the thirteen colonies want? ______

7. Who was George Washington? ______

8. Why do many new immigrants come to the United States? ______

What Do You Think?

9. Why do you think immigrants are coming to the United States now? ______

10. When did you arrive in the United States? ______

11. Are you living in the United States permanently? ______

12. Are there more opportunities here than in other countries? ______

Vocabulary Practice

▸EXERCISE 19

A. Read the whole paragraph first. Then complete the paragraph with the simple past tense form of the verbs in the box. You may use some verbs more than once.

be	arrive	want	form	celebrate	feel	write	become

The first Americans ____________________ Native American Indians. The first European immigrants ____________________ in Jamestown, Virginia, in 1607. The African slaves ____________________ in chains by ship. Later, many other immigrants arrived. The immigrants ____________________ thirteen colonies under England. The people of the thirteen colonies ____________________ that they were mistreated by England, and they ____________________ independence. The colonies ____________________ their independence on July 4, 1776. The new Americans ____________________ the Declaration of Independence. George Washington ____________________ the first president of the United States. There ____________________ thirteen stars and stripes on the first United States flag.

B. Choose five of the words from the box above to write questions to ask your classmates.

Example: *When did you arrive in the United States?*

1. ____________________
2. ____________________
3. ____________________
4. ____________________
5. ____________________

▶EXERCISE 20 Match the words with the description.

1. colonies ______
2. England ______
3. immigrants ______
4. independence ______
5. Jamestown ______
6. president ______
7. slaves ______
8. U.S. Census ______
9. *Mayflower* ______
10. equal ______

a. the ship that brought Europeans in 1607
b. people who come to a new country to live
c. The first one was in 1790.
d. the leader of the United States
e. where the first European immigrants came from
f. where the first European immigrants arrived
g. what the colonies wanted from England
h. what the immigrants formed in the United States
i. the same as other people
j. African people brought to America against their will

Reading Charts and Graphs

▶EXERCISE 21 A. Study the chart about U.S. immigration.

Immigration to the United States

Years	1500s	1607	1700s	1776	1790	1841–1860	1850	1880–1918
Nationalities	Mexican immigrants in the Southwest	First European immigrants from England	German, English, and Scots Irish	Approximately 20% of United States population was slaves	United States population was 5 million* (750,000 slaves)	3.5 million Irish, German, English, French, and Swiss	Chinese and Japanese immigrants	15 million Italians, Russians, Poles, and Hungarians

*U.S. Census, 1790.

B. Answer the questions about the chart.

1. What immigrants arrived in the United States in the 1700s? ______________________
2. When was the U.S. population five million people? ______________________
3. What immigrants arrived in 1850? ______________________
4. In what years did fifteen million people arrive? ______________________
5. When was the first U.S. census? ______________________

Expansion Activities

▸ Activity 1 Word Search *Find the words listed below in the word search.*

AGRICULTURE ARTIFACT ASTRONOMY
BATTLE CENSUS CHEROKEE
COTTON IGLOO LOOM
MIGRATE OWE PAPOOSE
FREEDOM STRIPES SURVIVE
TOBACCO

E	C	V	E	E	L	T	T	A	B	E	R	Y	A	M
E	R	O	I	C	A	N	I	S	R	L	S	A	N	I
M	M	I	T	G	R	A	N	U	T	O	I	A	D	N
O	S	D	E	T	M	Z	T	S	A	O	R	Y	W	Y
C	W	Y	A	Y	O	L	V	N	O	M	M	P	M	S
C	S	P	R	E	U	N	D	E	P	W	A	O	X	T
A	O	J	T	C	V	I	D	C	Z	P	N	C	R	R
B	O	M	I	G	R	A	T	E	O	O	C	B	S	I
O	L	R	F	M	T	F	Z	O	R	O	H	V	S	P
T	G	O	A	O	L	W	S	T	E	X	E	U	N	E
A	I	I	C	D	D	E	S	K	W	I	R	G	R	S
E	C	C	T	E	V	A	C	P	O	V	O	A	C	I
B	P	Y	J	E	L	D	M	R	I	Z	K	I	P	K
U	F	H	K	R	T	H	E	V	P	Y	E	W	K	H
V	R	U	B	F	E	X	E	W	W	U	E	D	V	C

▸ **Activity 2 Write Your Own Story** *Read the story about Nicholas, who came to the United States in 1842.*

I was born Nils Peter Vvedin in Vestebek, Sweden, in 1822. When I was twenty years old, I sailed with my cousin, who was the captain of a ship, to New York City. When we arrived in New York, I fell from the mast of the ship and was taken to a hospital on Manhattan Island. While I was recovering from my injuries, the ship returned to Sweden without me. I knew a little about cloth, so I got a job as a cloth cutter in a company owned by some Irish people and changed my name to Nicholas Peter Wedin. Several years later, I met an Irish girl named Katherine Riley. Katherine came to the United States with her mother and brother to look for her father, who had come a few years earlier to look for a job to feed his family in Ireland. He wrote several letters back home, and then his family never heard from him again. When they came to the United States, people told them that he had joined the army because he couldn't find a job. The United States was at war against Mexico. At the Army headquarters, they were told that he died in Mexico. Then Katherine and I met, and we were married. We had ten children and a beautiful life together.

Write the story of how you came to the United States. When did you come? What were your plans? Where did you live? Did you work or study when you came? Who did you meet? Include interesting details about your life in the United States. Use your notes from page 83 to help you. Then share your story with your classmates.

____

____

____

____

____

____

____

If you want to review vocabulary and complete additional activities related to this chapter, go to the *Read to Succeed 2* Web site at http://esl.college.hmco.com/students.

Vocabulary List

Adjectives
advanced
ago
elaborate
first
low-level
organized
Adjectives of Nationality, Tribe, or Origin
African
Asian
Cherokee
Chinese
English
European
German
Hungarian
Irish
Italian
Native American
Scottish
Swiss
Wampanoag

Adverbs
exactly
probably
south

Nouns
anthropologist
artifact
astronomy
attitude
bald eagle
battle
black slave
brave
census
chain
chart
civilization
codex/codices
colony/colonies
cotton
descendant
economic depression
factory/factories
flag
freedom
future
igloo
immigrant
migration
moccasin
mound
opportunity/opportunities
papoose
part
past
peace council
persecution
plantation
power
president
reservation
ship
skin
slave
society/societies
star
stripe
symbol
theft
thousands
tip
tobacco
tribe
will
zero
Proper Nouns
Africa
Alaska
Americas
Asia
Bering Strait
Bolivia
Canada
Declaration of Independence
Ellis Island
England
Guatemala
Hungary
Indian
Jamestown
Liberty Bell
Mayflower
Mexico
Native American
New York
Poland
Russia
South America
Statue of Liberty
Virginia
Washington, George

Prepositions
before
between
from
of
on
throughout
under
with

Verbs
arrive
blend
buy
contribute
develop
die
disagree
discover
fight
form
have
help
introduce
know
last
live
migrate
mistreat
move
need
owe
sell
separate
settle
sign
survive
thank
walk
want
win

CHAPTER 6

Americans and Their Leaders

Reading 1 Democracy in Action

Before You Read

▸**EXERCISE 1 Discuss these questions with a partner or small group.**

1. Who is the president of the United States now?
2. Is the president a Democrat or a Republican?
3. Who is the governor of the state where you live?

▶EXERCISE 2 Look at the diagram and answer the questions with a partner. Then write the branch of government that the question refers to.

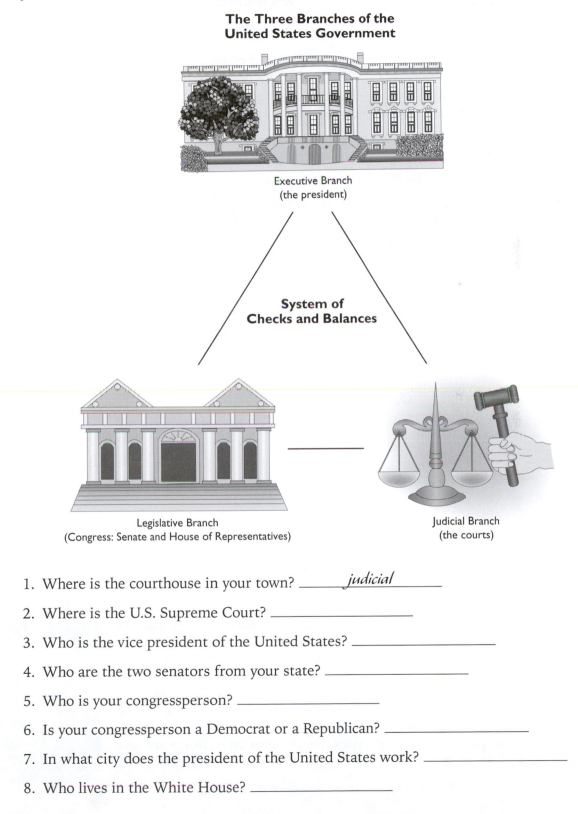

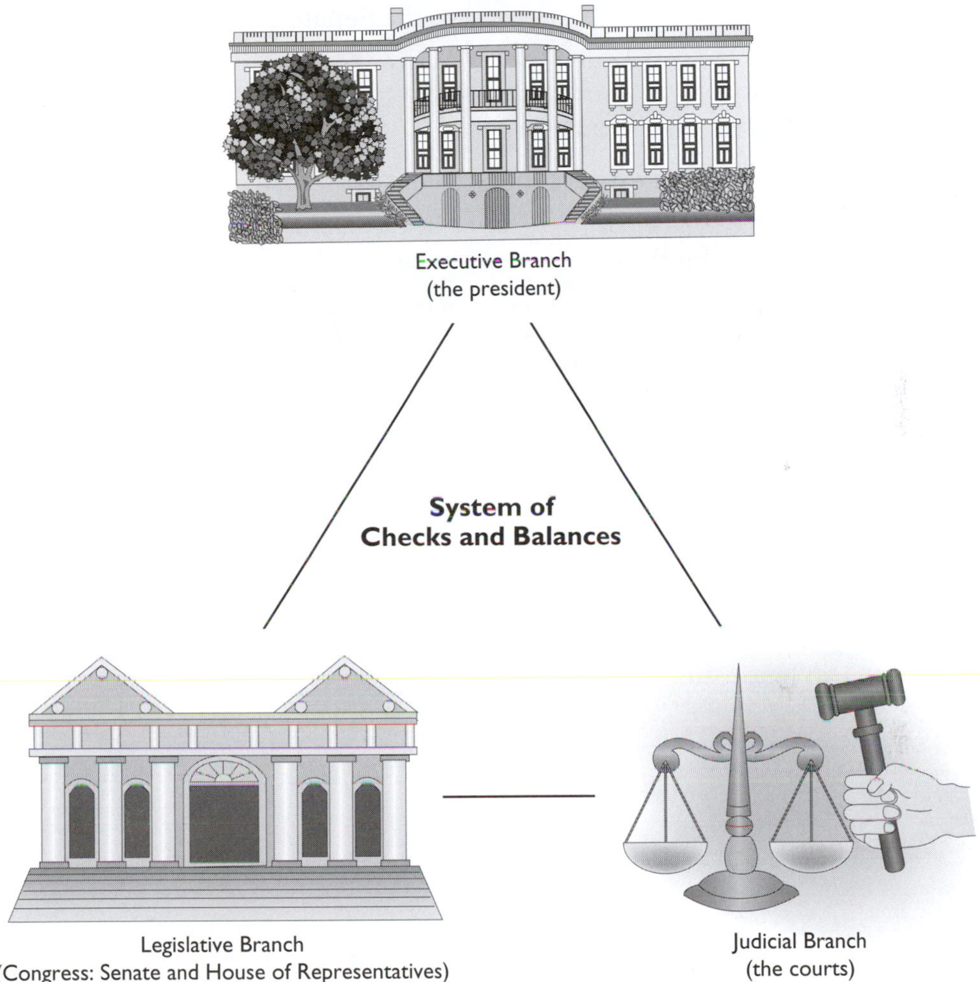

1. Where is the courthouse in your town? *judicial*
2. Where is the U.S. Supreme Court? ____________
3. Who is the vice president of the United States? ____________
4. Who are the two senators from your state? ____________
5. Who is your congressperson? ____________
6. Is your congressperson a Democrat or a Republican? ____________
7. In what city does the president of the United States work? ____________
8. Who lives in the White House? ____________

▸EXERCISE 3 Match the words with the definitions.

1. citizen ____
2. senator ____
3. U.S. Congress ____

a. a member of the U.S. Senate
b. a native or naturalized person of a country
c. the Senate and the House of Representatives

Words from the Reading*

candidate	**congressperson**	**senator**
citizen	**court**	**U.S. Congress**
Congress	**election**	**vote**

*Your teacher can help you understand these words and others listed at the end of the chapter and on the Web site at http://esl.college.hmco.com/students.

▸EXERCISE 4 Scan the reading and answer these questions.

1. What do you predict the reading will be about? ____________________

____

2. Who can be president of the United States? ____________________

____

3. How is the U.S. government divided? ____________________

____

Read to learn about the U.S. government and U.S. elections.*

Democracy in Action

The Branches of Government

In 1787 the writers of the U.S. Constitution divided the U.S. government into three parts, or branches: the **judicial** (courts), the **legislative** (U.S. Congress: Senate and House of Representatives), and the **executive** (the president and the vice president). The **Founding Fathers** wanted the three branches to be equal. This is called the separation of powers. They didn't want one branch to be too strong, and this system is called checks and balances. The U.S. government still has this division into three branches. There are elections for congresspersons every two years, for president every four years, and for senators every six years. Each of the fifty states has two senators in

Washington, D.C. The number of congresspersons a state has is based on the population of the state; the bigger the population, the more congresspersons. California has the most congresspersons (fifty-three) because it has a bigger population than any other state.

Voting in America

In a democracy like the United States, people vote for their leaders. This is called a representative government. Voting in an election in the United States is a very important right, and every person's vote counts. The American people decide who wins elections. Americans vote for local, state, and national candidates. There is an election for president every four years. The major candidates are always Republicans or Democrats. In the year 2000, the election for president was a very close vote, but George Bush won. The state of Florida's votes, counted last, decided the next president. The U.S. Supreme Court also participated in the decision. That same year, Americans also voted for members of Congress: senators and congresspersons. There are also state and local elections every year.

There are several **requirements** and rules about voting. Today, all U.S. citizens can vote if they are eighteen, but this was not always true. African American men received the right to vote in the 1860s, but they were kept from voting through **Jim Crow** laws and **segregation.** It was not until the 1960s that African Americans could freely exercise their right to vote. Women could not vote until 1922! Before 1971, young people under twenty-one years old could be soldiers but could not vote. Immigrants can vote, but they must first become U.S. citizens. Immigrants must also know some English to be able to vote. A citizen should read about the candidates and issues before an election. Everyone must register to vote before an election. People can vote at **designated** places in their community, or they can vote by mail.

designated	specific
executive	the branch of government concerned with putting laws into effect or managing the country
Founding Fathers	members of the convention that drafted the U.S. Constitution in 1787
Jim Crow	practices of unfairness and inequality against African Americans
judicial	relating to courts of the law
legislative	relating to making laws
requirement	a thing that is needed; a necessity
segregation	the act of separating or isolating from others

*Related class to take or visit: political science.

Comprehension

▸EXERCISE 5 Write T (true) or F (false) for each statement.

______ 1. The U.S. Congress has three branches.

______ 2. Candidates for government office are usually Democrat or Republican.

______ 3. The writers of the Constitution divided the government in 2000.

______ 4. The three branches are the judicial, national, and local.

______ 5. Judicial includes the president and the vice president.

______ 6. There are two senators for each state.

______ 7. There is an election for president every two years.

______ 8. The division of government is called the separation of powers.

______ 9. The legislative branch is the president and vice president.

______ 10. In a representative government, the people elect the candidate.

▸EXERCISE 6 Circle the letter of the main idea for each paragraph.

Paragraph 1:

a. There are three branches of government.
b. The president is the executive branch.
c. Democrats win every election.

Paragraph 2:

a. Senators are elected every six years.
b. The 2000 election was very close.
c. Voting is a key part of a democracy.

Paragraph 3:

a. Twenty-one-year-old people can vote.
b. Learning English is important.
c. There are requirements and rules for voting.

▶EXERCISE 7 Circle the letter of the correct answer.

1. Voting in the United States is an important _____.
   a. branch b. right c. election
2. The major political parties are the _____.
   a. senators b. candidates c. Democrats and Republicans
3. Senators and congresspersons are part of _____.
   a. Congress b. the Senate c. House of Representatives
4. In 1787 the writers of the _____ divided the government into three parts.
   a. branches b. Constitution c. Congress
5. The executive branch is the _____.
   a. courts b. president c. Congress
6. There are _____ states in the United States.
   a. 13 b. 100 c. 50
7. Each state has _____ senators.
   a. two b. five c. ten
8. The number of congresspersons in each state depends on the _____.
   a. money b. age c. population
9. A person who _____ can't vote.
   a. is not yet eighteen years old b. is a citizen c. is twenty-one years old
10. A citizen must _____ to vote before election day.
    a. register b. be a Democrat c. be over twenty-one years old
11. Elections for congresspersons are every _____.
    a. four years b. two years c. six years
12. The Founding Fathers wrote the _____ in 1787.
    a. branches b. Constitution c. judicial

▶EXERCISE 8 Read the questions and answer them orally with your teacher. Then answer them orally with a classmate. At home, write the answers for homework. Answer in complete sentences.

About the Reading

1. How often are elections for president held? ______________________________

   ____

2. What are the two major political parties in the United States? ______________

   ____

3. What are the three branches of government? ______________________________

   ____

4. In what year was the Constitution written? ______________________________

   ____

5. How old must a person be to vote in the United States? ____________________

   ____

6. Who can and cannot vote in the United States? __________________________

   ____

Questions for Discussion

7. Do you think the United States has a good system of government? Why or why not?

   ____

8. How is the government in your native country the same as or different from the U.S. government? ____

   ____

9. Do you think voting is important? Why or why not? ______________________

   ____

10. Do you want to be a citizen of the United States? Explain. ________________

    ____

11. Do you want to stay in the United States? Explain why. __________________

    ____

12. Are there good candidates for president in your native country? ___________

    ____

Vocabulary Practice

▶EXERCISE 9 Write the word from the reading that is similar in meaning (a synonym) to the underlined word.

1. Every individual's vote is important. (paragraph 2) ____________
2. The U.S. Supreme Court took part in the decision. (paragraph 2) ____________
3. A person must be familiar with English. (paragraph 3) ____________
4. You have to register before you can vote. (paragraph 3) ____________
5. In 1787 the U.S. government was separated into three branches. (paragraph 1) ____________
6. They desired a balanced government. (paragraph 1) ____________
7. They wanted the three branches to be the same. (paragraph 1) ____________
8. We still have this separation today. (paragraph 1) ____________

▶EXERCISE 10 Match the words with the descriptions.

1. candidate ____	a. There are two for each state.
2. Congress ____	b. This is held the day people vote.
3. election ____	c. He or she lives in the White House.
4. president ____	d. A person running for political office.
5. senator ____	e. Put an X by a candidate's name.
6. vote ____	f. Senate and the House of Representatives.
7. political parties ____	g. Judicial, executive, and legislative.
8. representative government ____	h. The legal age to vote.
9. three branches ____	i. Democrat and Republican.
10. eighteen years old ____	j. The people choose.

Grammar Hints: Modal Auxiliaries

Modal auxiliaries are helping verbs used before another verb. The common modal auxiliaries are as follows:

will (future)
might (maybe, possibly, probably)
should (a suggestion or obligation: "ought to")
must (have to)
can (able to—present tense)
could (able to—past tense)
may (ask or give permission)
can't (negative)
couldn't (negative)

In affirmative and negative sentences, the correct order is this:

Modal Auxiliary + Verb (Affirmative)
You should vote on election day.
I must register to vote.

Modal Auxiliary + *not* + Verb (Negative)
An eighteen-year-old could not vote before.
She is only sixteen, so she may not vote.

Note that the endings of the verbs do not change.

▶EXERCISE 11 Complete each sentence with an appropriate modal auxiliary from the list above. More than one may be correct. You may use the modals more than once.

1. She ___*can*___ vote now because she is a U.S. citizen.
2. I ____________ not speak English two years ago, but now I can speak it well.
3. A candidate for president ____________ be a citizen.
4. We ____________ listen to the candidates before the election.
5. She is sure that she ____________ vote for a woman for president next time.
6. He doesn't know yet. He ____________ vote for a man or a woman.
7. I am not sure. I ____________ listen to the candidate's speech on television.
8. The man asked, "____________ I register to vote here?"
9. Mom, ____________ I go to the movies with my friends tomorrow?
10. Yes, son. You ____________ go after you do your homework.

Reading 2 When the President Dies

Before You Read

▶EXERCISE 12 Discuss these questions with a partner or small group.

1. What happens if the leader of a country dies?
2. What countries do you know of where a president died while in office?
3. How do people feel when the president of their country dies?
4. What do you know about Abraham Lincoln?
5. Who was John F. Kennedy?
6. Who are the president and vice president now?

▶EXERCISE 13 Write the letter of the correct definition.

1. assassinated ______ a. the president's airplane
2. motorcade ______ b. a line of cars moving slowly with important people inside
3. *Air Force One* ______ c. a leader is murdered

▸EXERCISE 14 Look at the pictures and write the correct letter next to each sentence.

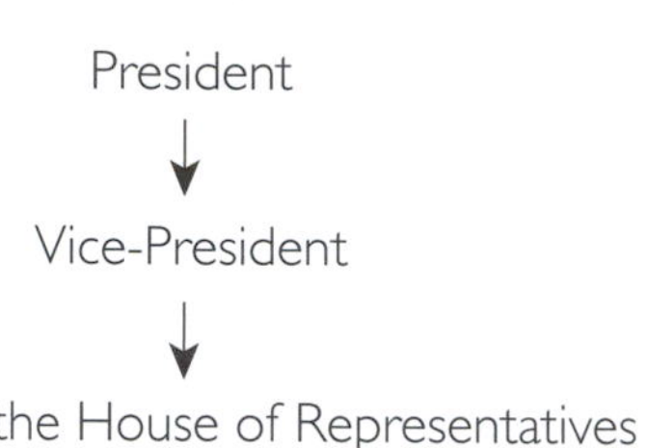

A.

B.

C.

E.

Daily Times

10 cents November 22, 1963

JFK Killed in Dallas!

Vice President Johnson Now President!

D.

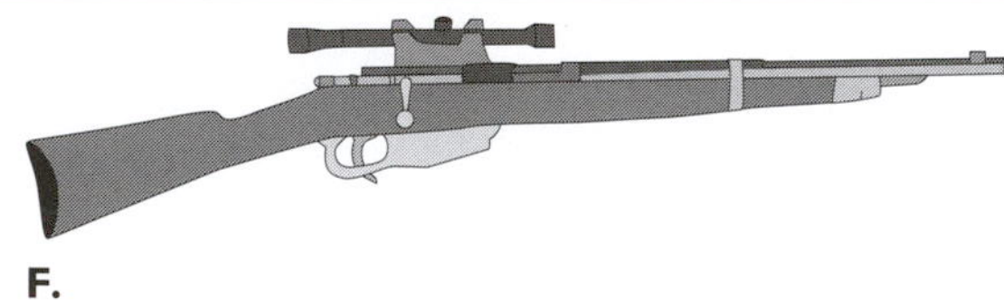

F.

1. How many presidents have died in office? ____________________
2. Where did John F. Kennedy die? ____________________
3. What is the name of the president's airplane? ____________________
4. What is the name of the system that determines the next president when the president dies? ____________________
5. Who killed John F. Kennedy? ____________________
6. Who was the vice president when President Kennedy died? ____________________

▸EXERCISE 15 Scan the reading and answer these questions.

1. Who becomes president if the president of the United States dies in office? ______________________________

2. Is there a new election? ______________________________

3. Who is third in line? ______________________________

4. How many U.S. presidents died in office? ______________________________

5. Who was John F. Kennedy? ______________________________

6. What is presidential succession? ______________________________

7. Who is in the picture on page 102? ______________________________

8. What two presidents died in office? ______________________________

Words from the Reading*

Air Force One	in office
assassinate	motorcade
government	vice president

*Your teacher can help you understand these words and others listed at the end of the chapter and on the Web site at http://esl.college.hmco.com/students.

Read to find out about presidential succession.

When the President Dies

What happens if the President of the United States dies? From 1789 to 1963, eight U.S. presidents died in office for different reasons. Ronald Reagan was shot in 1981 but lived. The president is always in danger, so the **Secret Service** must protect him. Sometimes Secret Service protection is not enough. If the president dies, who is the next president? Who is third in line? Is there a new election? Is there a new government? The answers to these questions are in the U.S. Constitution. The last time a president was killed was in 1963, when someone assassinated President John F. Kennedy. The country was in danger and needed a new president, but the government did not fall.

John F. Kennedy (JFK) was forty-three years old when he was elected as the thirty-fifth president of the United States in 1960. He was young, a Democrat, and popular with many people. President Kennedy, his wife, and the governor of Texas and his wife were in a motorcade in a convertible on November 22, 1963, in Dallas, Texas. At 12:30 PM, one or more people shot the president as he was riding in a car. The governor of Texas was also shot but lived. President Kennedy died from a shot or shots to his head and neck. Who was the person or group that killed President Kennedy? Forty years later, we still don't know for sure. The country was shocked, sad, and nervous. Some people thought that the country was in danger, but the government did not fall. At 2:38 PM, on *Air Force One,* the president's plane, the vice president, Lyndon B. Johnson, became the new president. When the plane arrived in Washington, D.C., the country had a new president.

The system of choosing the next president is called **presidential succession.** After President Franklin Roosevelt died in office, the Presidential Succession Act of 1947 was written into the U.S. Constitution. The U.S. government must follow this system. If the president dies, the vice president becomes the next president. If the vice president also dies, the **Speaker of the House** of Representatives must become president. The president of the Senate is next in line. Sixteen people are on the list after the president! Only people on the list can become president. The government started keeping a vice-presidential succession list in 1967. If the president or government is in danger from a terrorist act, as happened in September 2001, the U.S. government moves away from Washington, D.C., and the president moves out of the White House. They move to a secret location underground, but the government continues. The U.S. Constitution ensures that the leadership of the country is in place at all times.

presidential succession	the order of people who become president if the president dies
Secret Service	a branch of the U.S. Treasury Department whose work includes the protection of the president
Speaker of the House	the leader of the House of Representatives; third in line to be president

Comprehension

▸EXERCISE 16 Write T (true) or F (false) for each statement.

_____ 1. If the president of the United States dies, the government falls.

_____ 2. The U.S. Constitution has a presidential succession plan in it.

_____ 3. From 1769 to 1963, ten presidents died in office.

_____ 4. In 1963 someone or some group assassinated President Kennedy.

_____ 5. Kennedy died in Dallas, Texas.

_____ 6. When he died, Kennedy was seventy-five years old.

_____ 7. After Johnson died, Kennedy became president.

_____ 8. The Speaker of the House of Representatives is third in line.

_____ 9. The president's plane is *Star Wars One*.

_____ 10. When Kennedy died, Americans were nervous and sad.

_____ 11. Ronald Reagan was shot in 2004.

_____ 12. There is no vice presidential succession.

_____ 13. The U.S. government is always in Washington, D.C.

_____ 14. The governor of Texas became president in 1963.

▶EXERCISE 17 Circle the letter of the correct answer.

1. If the president of the United States dies, who is next in line?
   a. the Speaker of the House b. the vice president c. a senator
2. Where can we find presidential succession?
   a. the Constitution b. the election c. the courts
3. How many U.S. presidents died in office from 1789 to 2003?
   a. none b. eight c. four
4. Who was the last U.S. president to die in office?
   a. Kennedy b. Reagan c. Lincoln
5. When did President Kennedy die?
   a. 1865 b. 1988 c. 1963
6. Where was Kennedy when he died?
   a. in his office b. on *Air Force One* c. in a motorcade
7. Who killed JFK?
   a. No one knows for sure. b. Only the government knows. c. The police know.
8. Where was the vice president at 2:38 PM on November 22, 1963?
   a. in Washington b. in Pennsylvania c. on *Air Force One*
9. Who is the next in line after the vice president?
   a. a senator b. the Speaker of the House of Representatives c. a congressperson
10. How many people are on the list of presidential succession?
    a. three b. ten c. sixteen

▶EXERCISE 18 Write the main idea for each paragraph.

1. Paragraph 1: ______________________________.
2. Paragraph 2: ______________________________.
3. Paragraph 3: ______________________________.

▶**EXERCISE 19 Read the questions and answer them orally with your teacher. Then answer the questions orally with a classmate. At home, write the answers for homework. Answer in complete sentences.**

1. When and how did President John F. Kennedy die? ____________________
____
2. Who assassinated John F. Kennedy? ____________________
____
3. Who was the vice president when JFK was assassinated? ____________________
____
4. What happens to the government if there is a serious terrorist act in Washington, D.C.? ____________________
____
5. Who is next in line if the vice president dies, too? ____________________
____
6. Why is presidential succession a good idea? ____________________
____
7. Why do you think the government did not fall in 1963? ____________________
____
8. Why do you think Americans were nervous on November 22, 1963? ____________________
____
9. Who does the Secret Service protect? ____________________
____
10. Describe President Kennedy. ____________________
____
11. What is *Air Force 1*? ____________________
____
12. What happened in the United States in September 2001? ____________________
____

Vocabulary Practice

▶EXERCISE 20 Complete the sentences with the correct word or phrase from the box.

Air Force One	vice president	died in office	terrorist act
Speaker	killed	motorcade	presidential succession
shot	dies	protects	assassinated

1. When ______________ arrived at the airport in Washington, D.C., on November 22, 1963, there was a new president.
2. Eight U.S. presidents ______________ from 1789 to 1988.
3. The ______________ of the House is third in line after the vice president.
4. Kennedy died while riding in a ______________ on November 22, 1963.
5. No one knows for sure who ______________ John F. Kennedy.
6. The name of the system for choosing another president is ______________.
7. If there is serious danger from a ______________, the government moves away from Washington, D.C.
8. Lyndon Johnson was ______________ and next in line when Kennedy died.
9. The Secret Service ______________ the president.
10. Someone ______________ JFK in Dallas, Texas, in 1963.
11. The president and the governor were ______________.
12. If the president ______________ in office, the vice president becomes president.

▶EXERCISE 21 Read the whole paragraph. Then complete the paragraph with words from the box. Use each word only once.

assassins	violence	caused	right	citizens
Constitution	believe	protection	Founding Fathers	protect
violent	assassinated			

A Right, or an Invitation to Violence?

When the ________________ wrote the ________________, they included the right of American ________________ to bear arms. Some people, like members of the National Rifle Association (NRA), think that keeping arms in homes for ________________ is very American. They also think that this constitutional ________________ is an important and basic freedom for all Americans. Their motto, or popular expression, is "Guns don't kill people; people kill people." After JFK was assassinated in 1963, other well-known political leaders were shot or killed by ________________ in the 1960s. Robert Kennedy, JFK's brother, was shot to death in Los Angeles in 1968. Martin Luther King Jr. was an important civil rights leader who was gunned down by assassins in Memphis, Tennessee, in the same year. Many people today ________________ that guns have ________________ and continue to cause too much ________________ and killing in America, especially in our cities. They say that too many innocent victims die each year as a result of killings with guns or gun accidents. When an American leader is ________________ by a person with a gun, some Americans become antigun. Americans who are pro-gun say that people are ________________, not guns, because guns ________________ us from dangerous people.

Expansion Activities

▶ Activity 1 Register to Vote *Complete this sample voter registration form. Ask your teacher or find out on your own where you can obtain actual voter registration forms in your community.*

Voter Registration Application

Are you a citizen of the United States of America? ☐ Yes ☐ No Will you be 18 years old on or before election day? ☐ Yes ☐ No **If you checked "No" in response to either of these questions, do not complete form.** (Please see state-specific instructions for rules regarding eligibility to register prior to age 18.)	This space for office use only.

1	(Circle one) Mr. Mrs. Miss Ms.	Last Name	First Name	Middle Name(s)	(Circle one) Jr Sr II III IV
2	Home Address	Apt. or Lot #	City/Town	State	Zip Code
3	Address Where You Get Your Mail If Different From Above		City/Town	State	Zip Code

4	Date of Birth ___ / ___ / ___ Month Day Year	5	Telephone Number (optional)	6	ID Number - (See Item 6 in the instructions for your state)
7	Choice of Party (see item 7 in the instructions for your State)	8	Race or Ethnic Group (see item 8 in the instructions for your State)		

9	I have reviewed my state's instructions and I swear/affirm that: ■ I am a United States citizen ■ I meet the eligibility requirements of my state and subscribe to any oath required. ■ The information I have provided is true to the best of my knowledge under penalty of perjury. If I have provided false information, I may be fined, imprisoned, or (if not a U.S. citizen) deported from or refused entry to the United States.	Please sign full name (or put mark) Date: ___ / ___ / ___ Month Day Year

▶ Activity 2 Bingo *Draw a bingo grid like this one on a piece of paper.*

In each space, write one word from the vocabulary you learned in this chapter (nine words total). Then your teacher will read definitions of some of the words from the chapter. If you have a word that matches the definition your teacher reads, mark it with an X. When you have three Xs in a row, horizontally, vertically, or diagonally, call out, "Bingo!"

Vocabulary List

Adjectives

balanced
bigger
close
designated
enough
equal
executive
judicial
last
legislative
local
major
national
presidential
representative
shocked
terrorist
third
thirty-fifth

Adverbs

freely
slowly
still

Nouns

act
assassin
branch
candidate
checks and balances
citizen
congressperson
convertible
court
decision
division
election
government
line
motorcade
plane
political party/parties
population
president
presidential succession
protection
requirement
segregation
senator
shot
speech
state
system
vice president
vote
voting

Proper Nouns

Air Force One
American
Congress
Dallas, Texas
Democrat
Florida
Founding Fathers
House of Representatives
Jim Crow
Johnson, Lyndon B.
Kennedy, John F.
November
President
Reagan, Ronald
Republican
Secret Service
Senate
Speaker of the House
Supreme Court
U.S. Constitution
Washington, D.C.

Verbs

decide
elect
follow
register

Modal Auxiliaries

can
can't
could
couldn't
have to
may
must
should

Verbs—Simple Past

assassinated
based
decided
did
didn't
died
divided
elected
killed
lived
needed
participated
voted
won

If you want to review vocabulary and complete additional activities related to this chapter, go to the *Read to Succeed 2* Web site at http://esl.college.hmco.com/students.

CHAPTER 7

Continents and Population

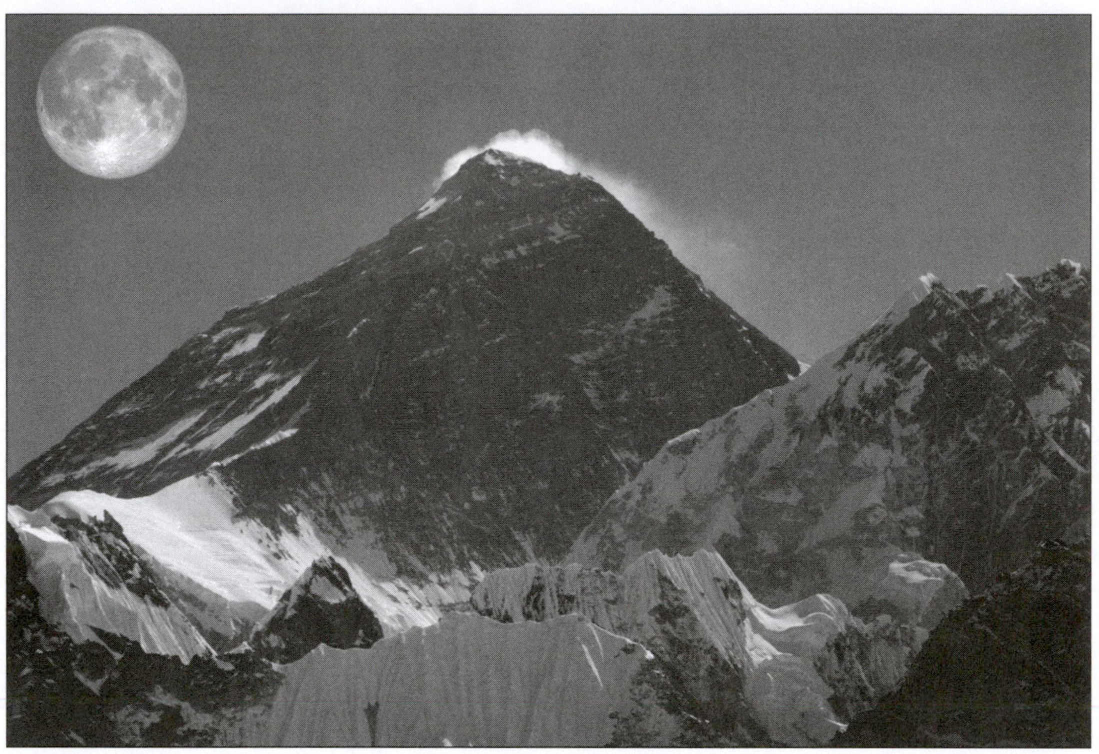

Reading 1 Continents, Ancient and Modern

Before You Read

EXERCISE 1 Discuss these questions with a partner or a small group.

1. What are the names of the five continents shown on the map below?
2. What continent do you live on?*
3. What two continents are not on this map?

*Cultural note: Some students are taught that there are five continents (the Americas are one continent, and Australia is part of Asia); other students learn that there are six continents, with Australia separate from Asia. In the United States, students are taught that there are seven continents: South America, North America, Australia, Asia, Europe, Africa, and Antarctica.

▶EXERCISE 2 Look at the map of five of Earth's continents and answer the questions.

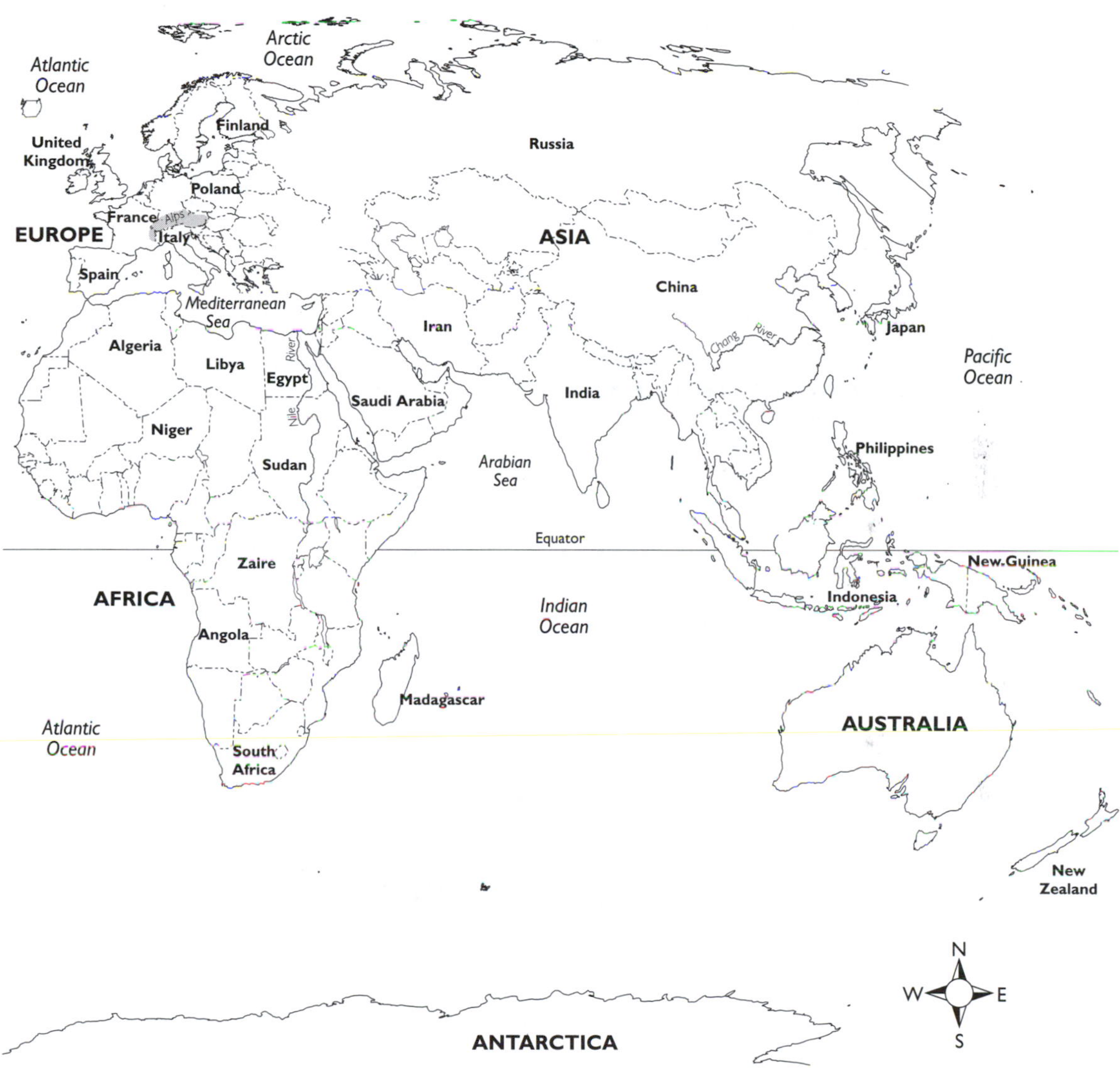

1. What is the name of the ocean west of Africa and Europe? ____________________
2. What continent is north of Africa? (Name one.) ____________________
3. What continent is Japan part of? ____________________
4. Which continent is the smallest? ____________________
5. Which continent on this map is the coldest? ____________________

▶EXERCISE 3 Write T (true) or F (false) for each statement.

_____ 1. Asia and Africa are countries.

_____ 2. The Nile and the Amazon are rivers.

_____ 3. The Rockies and the Alps are states.

Words from the Reading*

continent **mountain range**
equator **river**
landmass

*Your teacher can help you understand these words and others listed at the end of the chapter and on the Web site at http://esl.college.hmco.com/students.

▶EXERCISE 4 Discuss these questions with a partner.

1. How many continents are there?
2. What are the names of the two large oceans?
3. What are the names of some rivers and mountains?

Read to learn about world geography.*

Continents, Ancient and Modern

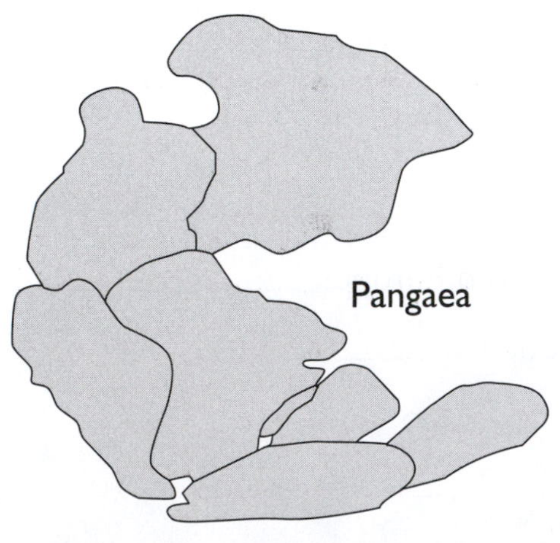

Pangaea

The earth is made up of seven large **landmasses** called continents: Africa, Asia, Australia, Antarctica, North America, South America, and Europe. The planet **Earth** is 30 percent land and 70 percent water. In square miles, Australia is the smallest continent, and Asia is the largest. The earth is always changing and moving. It has eight large **tectonic plates** and a few smaller plates on its crust. The seven continents are on this **surface** and can move with the tectonic plates. There is very hot **magma** in the center of the earth. The heat from the magma moves up to the crust very slowly. Magma on the surface of the crust is called lava. Sometimes volcanoes or earthquakes move the plates and continents. One of the most interesting and most beautiful places in the world is the Hawaiian Islands. These islands

*Related classes to take or visit: geography and anthropology.

were formed by underwater volcanoes. The continents near the equator are the hottest, and those continents farthest from the equator are the coldest.

Geologists think the earth is five billion years old and that more than 300 million years ago, there was only one continent, Pangaea. Geologists say that about 180 million years ago, little by little, Pangaea broke into two large continents: Gondwanaland and Laurasia. Gondwanaland was made up of what later became South America, Africa, Antarctica, India, and Australia. Laurasia was made up of North America, Europe, and Asia. The two large continents began to break up further around 130 million years ago. When India crashed violently into Asia, the Himalaya Mountains formed, the highest mountains in the world. Australia moved north and away from Antarctica. Little by little, today's seven continents formed. Today, the continents are still moving slowly. Some geologists think that in 40–50 million years, North America and South America will be separate, and Australia will move north.

Most continents have at least one large mountain range and a long river. The mountain ranges are the Himalayas in Asia, the Great Dividing Range in Australia, the Alps in Europe, the Andes in South America, and the Rocky Mountains in North America. Mount Everest in the Himalayas is the tallest mountain in the world and the most difficult to climb. Africa does not have a large mountain range. Most continents also have a long river except Antarctica, one of the coldest places on Earth. Some of the longest rivers in the world are the Nile in Africa, the Amazon in South America, the Chang in China, the Ob in Russia, and the Missouri-Mississippi in the United States. The Nile and the Amazon are the longest rivers in the world. Geologists say that the seven large landmasses, their rivers, and their mountain ranges are always changing.

the earth or Earth	the planet on which human beings live
geologist	a scientist who specializes in geology (the study of the origin, history, and structure of the earth)
landmass	a large area of land
magma	the liquid rock material under Earth's surface
surface	the outermost layer or boundary of an object
tectonic plate	a large structural plate below the earth's surface

Reading Charts and Graphs

▸EXERCISE 5

A. Study the chart about mountain ranges and rivers.

Mountain Ranges and Rivers

Mountain Range		River		
Name	**Continent**	**Name**	**Length —Miles**	**Continent**
Alps	Europe	Amazon	4,000	South America
Andes	South America	Chang	3,964	Asia
Great Dividing Range	Australia	Missouri*	3,990	North America
Himalayas	Asia	Ob	3,362	Asia (Russia)
Rockies	North America	Nile	4,160	Africa
		Yangtze	3,200	Asia

*Missouri-Mississippi.

Source: Central Intelligence Agency (CIA), 2002.

B. Answer the questions about the chart.

1. Where is the highest mountain range in the world? ____________
2. Where is the Great Dividing Range? ____________
3. Which is the longest river? ____________
4. Which river is closest in length to the Nile River? ____________
5. What is the name of the mountain range in South America? ____________
6. Where are the Rocky Mountains? ____________
7. What is the name of the mountain range in Africa? ____________
8. Where is the Missouri-Mississippi River? ____________

Comprehension

▶EXERCISE 6 Write T (true) or F (false) for each statement.

_____ 1. There are four continents on Earth today.

_____ 2. Three hundred million years ago, there were seven continents.

_____ 3. Pangaea moved quickly five billion years ago.

_____ 4. The continents are not moving today.

_____ 5. Africa has a long mountain range.

_____ 6. The mountain range in North America is the Alps.

_____ 7. The long river in Africa is the Nile.

_____ 8. The Chang River is in Asia.

_____ 9. A continent is a large landmass.

_____ 10. The people who study the earth are zoologists.

▶EXERCISE 7 Circle the letter of the main idea for each paragraph.

Paragraph 1:

a. There are five continents.
b. There are seven rivers and mountain ranges.
c. There are seven large landmasses or continents.

Paragraph 2:

a. About 300 million years ago, there was a large population.
b. Geologists think that about five billion years ago, there was one continent that later broke apart.
c. Each continent has mountain ranges and long rivers.

Paragraph 3:

a. Most continents have a large mountain range and a long river.
b. Each mountain range has a large river.
c. Each continent has a large mountain range and a long river except Asia.

▸EXERCISE 8 Read the questions and answer them orally with your teacher. Then answer the questions orally with a classmate. At home, write the answers for homework. Answer in complete sentences.

1. How many continents were there 300 million years ago? ______________________

   ____

2. What continent is south of Asia? ______________________

   ____

3. What continent are the Alps in? ______________________

   ____

4. What do geologists study? ______________________

   ____

5. What is a continent? ______________________

   ____

6. What is the name of the ocean between North America and Europe? ______________________

   ____

7. Where is the longest river in the world, and what is its name? ______________________

   ____

8. What is the name of the continent south of Africa? ______________________

   ____

9. Which continent is the smallest? ______________________

   ____

10. Which is the highest mountain in the world, and where is it? ______________________

    ____

11. What continent does not have a mountain range? ______________________

    ____

12. What happened when India crashed into Asia? ______________________

    ____

Vocabulary Practice

▶EXERCISE 9 Circle the letter of the correct answer.

1. What is a large landmass called?

   a. mountain range b. a continent c. the earth

2. Who studies Earth's surface and features?

   a. physicists b. geologists c. politicians

3. The Rocky Mountains, Andes, Himalayas, and Great Dividing are ______.

   a. mountain ranges b. rivers c. continents

4. The Chang, Ob, Nile, and Amazon are ______.

   a. landmasses b. rivers c. mountains

5. What percentage of Earth is continents?

   a. 50% b. 30% c. 70%

6. On what continent is the Missouri-Mississippi River?

   a. Asia b. North America c. Africa

7. Where are the earth's highest mountains, the Himalayas?

   a. South America b. Europe c. Asia

8. What continent is south of Europe?

   a. Africa b. Asia c. South America

9. Three hundred million years ago,

   a. North and South America moved. b. Pangaea started to move. c. There was only one continent.

10. About 180 million years ago,

    a. India crashed into Asia. b. Pangaea broke into two large continents. c. Africa and Europe moved apart.

▶EXERCISE 10 Look at the map and the numbers; then fill in the blanks below with words from the box.

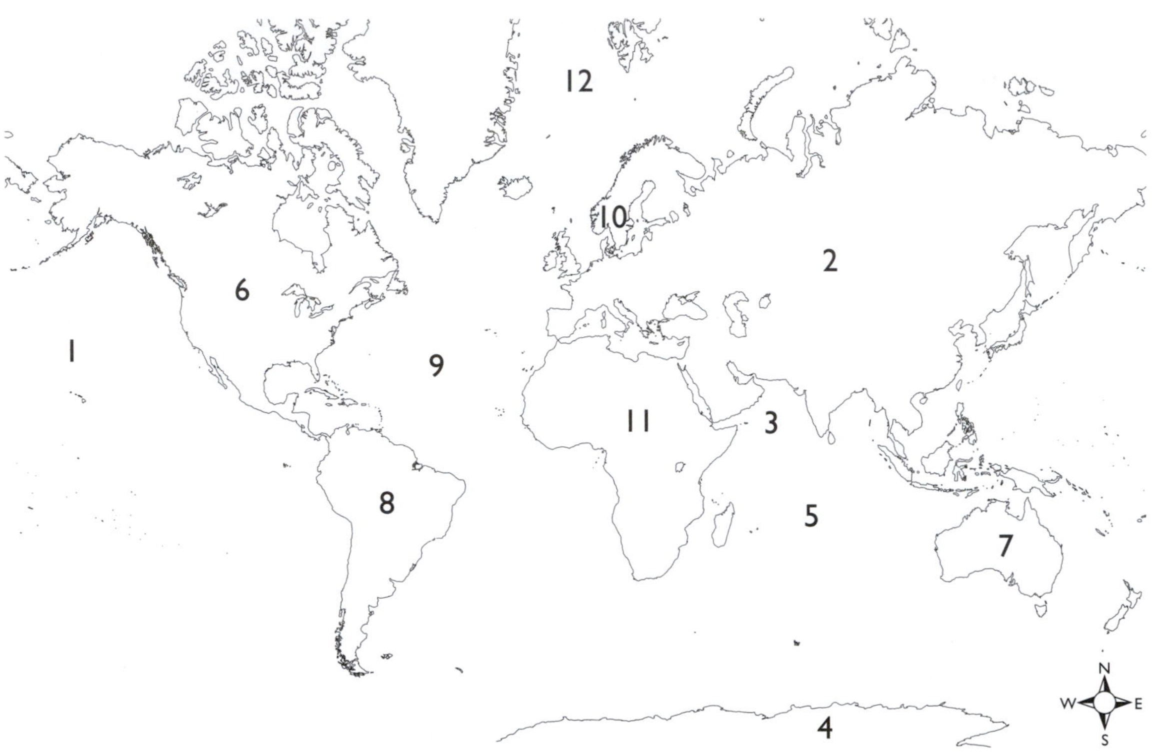

Pacific Ocean	North America	Indian Ocean	Africa
South America	Antarctica	Arctic Ocean	Europe
Asia	Atlantic Ocean	Australia	Arabian Sea

1. ____________________
2. ____________________
3. ____________________
4. ____________________
5. ____________________
6. ____________________
7. ____________________
8. ____________________
9. ____________________
10. ____________________
11. ____________________
12. ____________________

Grammar Hints: Superlative Adjectives

The superlative form of adjectives is used to compare three or more things, people, or places.

For adjectives of one or two syllables, add *-st* or *-est* according to these rules.

If the adjective ends in e, add *-st:*

large/largest

For other short adjectives, add *-est:*

cold/coldest, small/smallest, hot/hottest

For adjectives of three or more syllables, write *the most* or *the least* before the adjective:

the least interesting/the most interesting, the least expensive/the most expensive, the least incredible/the most incredible

---

▸EXERCISE 11 Complete each sentence with the superlative of the adjective in parentheses.

1. Australia is *the smallest* (small) continent in the world.
2. The Nile is ________ (long) river of all.
3. The Hawaiian Islands are one of ________ (beautiful) places in the world.
4. Mount Everest is ________ (high) mountain in the world and ________ (difficult) to climb.
5. Antarctica is one of ________ (cold) places on Earth.
6. Geography is one of ________ (interesting) subjects at school. I really like it.
7. Asia is ________ (large) continent.
8. Mountain climbing is one of ________ (incredible) sports in the world.
9. A desert is one of ________ places in summer.
10. Ice is one of ________ materials on earth.

Reading 2 Population and How It Affects the Earth

Before You Read

▶EXERCISE 12 Discuss these questions with a partner or small group.

1. What countries in the Americas are English-speaking?
2. What continent is Mexico on?
3. Is Cuba north or south of the United States?
4. Where is Central America on the map?

▶EXERCISE 13 Use the map on the next page and what you already know to answer the questions with a partner or a small group.

1. In which country do people speak Portuguese? ____________________
2. What countries are the hottest? Do you know why? ____________________
3. What two countries nearest the United States are Spanish-speaking?

   ____
4. About how many languages do people in the United States speak?

   ____
5. What continent is south of South America? ____________________
6. What area connects North and South America? ____________________
7. Which countries have the largest population? ____________________
8. What languages are spoken in the Caribbean countries? ____________________
9. What two states are separate from the other forty-eight states?

   ____
10. Where is Greenland? ____________________

Arctic Ocean
Greenland
NORTH AMERICA
Canada
United States
Atlantic Ocean
Mexico
Gulf of Mexico
Cuba
Dom. Republic
Caribbean Sea
CENTRAL AMERICA
Panama
Venezuela
Colombia
SOUTH AMERICA
Equator
Ecuador
Peru
Brazil
Bolivia
Pacific Ocean
Chile
Argentina
Uruguay
N
W
E
S
ANTARCTICA

The Americas

▸EXERCISE 14 Complete each sentence with a word from the "Words from the Reading."

1. Clean air, water, land, and forests are important ________________.
2. Two people who have different opinions ________________.
3. Water that is ________________ is dirty and polluted.

Words from the Reading*

contaminated	**issues**
disagree	**overpopulation**
estimate	**poverty**

*Your teacher can help you understand these words and others listed at the end of the chapter and on the Web site at http://esl.college.hmco.com/students.

Read to find out about population and what it does to the earth.*

Population and How It Affects the Earth

Geographers study population and how it affects conditions on Earth. They keep statistics (numbers) on the world's population. These statistics are not exact but are estimates because geographers cannot give us exact numbers for the future. Nevertheless, geographers use these statistics to make **predictions** about possible problems that overpopulation may cause.

The world's population is growing every day. In 1987 it was 5 billion people.* China was the biggest and the only country with a population of 1 billion. Geographers recorded that there were 220,000 new babies born every day. The population statistics for 1999 were very different.* The world's population was 6 billion—only 12 years later! China and India were the most **populous,** and each now has over 1 billion people. The United States has a population of 283,230,000. In the poorest countries, where many people live below the poverty level, there is not enough food,* the water is contaminated, and there is poor sanitation. Some countries are rich but still have many poor people. In some countries, 80 percent of the people are living below the poverty level.**

*United Nations, 2002.
**CIA, 2002.

Overpopulation causes other serious problems. One is global warming, which means that Earth is getting warmer. The richest and most industrialized countries produce the most **greenhouse gases** and pollution that go into the atmosphere and affect the earth's climate and temperature, causing global warming. Some poor countries are trying to become **industrialized.** Housing is another problem. A United Nations report on housing says that careless government **regulations** add to the problem of not enough housing, especially in cities.*** In addition, overpopulation helps cause the **extinction** of animals and plants and the disappearance of forests, wetlands, and other important **habitats.**

Countries around the world do not agree on how to solve problems caused by overpopulation. The United Nations held a conference on the earth's climate in Kyoto, Japan, in 1998. The countries that attended the conference wrote the Kyoto Protocol to protect the earth. As of September 2003, 119 countries have signed it, but the United States has not. The United Nations held an **environmental** conference in 2002 in South Africa to reduce poverty and protect the planet, but countries disagreed on how to do it. If the countries of the world are going to solve the issues of overpopulation, poverty, and greenhouse gases, all countries have to participate and try to agree.

Note: Related classes to take or visit: geography and anthropology.

environmental	having to do with surroundings and conditions that affect growth and development of living things
extinction	condition of no longer existing or living
geographer	someone who specializes in the study of Earth's surface and features
greenhouse gas	a gas forming around Earth that contributes to global warming
habitat	an area or a natural environment where animals or plants normally live or grow
industrialized	developed with industries
populous	heavily populated
prediction	something told in advance
regulation	a rule, order, or law

****Global Report on Human Settlements,* United Nations, March 1996.

Reading Charts and Graphs

►EXERCISE 15

A. Study the statistics about population.

Adding One Billion to the World's Population*

Years to Reach 1 Billion	Year	Population
	1804	1 billion
123	1927	2 billion
33	1960	3 billion
14	1974	4 billion
13	1987	5 billion
12	1999	6 billion

*United Nations estimate, 2002.

The World's Population in Millions*

Asia	3,672,342,000
Africa	793,627,000
Europe	727,504,000
South America**	518,809,000
North America	314,113,000
Oceania	30,521,000

*United Nations estimates, 2002.
**Includes the Caribbean countries.

Percentage of People Below the Poverty Level*

Country	Percentage
Zambia	86
Tajikistan	80
Madagascar	70
Mozambique	70
Rwanda	70
Venezuela	67
Iran	53

*CIA, 2002.

B. Answer the questions about the statistics provided in A.

1. In how many years did the world's population increase from one to two billion?

   ____

2. How long did it take for the population to increase from five to six billion?

   ____

3. Which continent has the biggest population? ____________________
4. Which continent has a bigger population, Europe or South America?

   ____

5. Which two countries have a poverty rate of 80 percent or more?

   ____

6. Of these seven countries, which one has the lowest poverty level?

   ____

7. On what continent are three of these countries? ____________________
8. Where did the poverty level statistics come from? ____________________

Comprehension

▸EXERCISE 16 Circle the letter of the correct answer. Look at the reading and at the charts in Exercise 15 for some answers.

1. Who keeps statistics about the world's population?
   a. politicians b. geographers c. engineers
2. Geographers make ______ about statistics for the future.
   a. predictions b. details c. numbers
3. The numbers that geographers give for the future are not exact but only ______.
   a. exact numbers b. figures c. estimates
4. What was the world's population in 1987?
   a. six million b. five billion c. seven million
5. How many new babies were born each day in 1987?
   a. 220,000 b. one million c. two billion
6. What was the world's population in 1999?
   a. five billion b. seven billion c. six billion
7. Which continent has the lowest population now?
   a. South America b. Asia c. Europe
8. Which country has the most people below the poverty level?
   a. Tajikistan b. Venezuela c. Zambia
9. Which continent has a population of almost 300 million?
   a. United States b. Europe c. South America
10. How many years did it take to move from two billion to three billion in population?
    a. 14 years b. 123 years c. 33 years

▸EXERCISE 17 Circle the letter of the main idea for each paragraph.

Paragraph 1:

a. Statistics are estimates.
b. Geographers study population.
c. Overpopulation causes problems.

Paragraph 2:

a. The world's population is growing.

b. People live below the poverty level in the poorest countries.

c. There is a big difference between the population in 1987 and 1999.

Paragraph 3:

a. Global warming means the earth is getting warmer.

b. Forests and wetlands are important habitats.

c. Overpopulation causes serious problems.

Paragraph 4:

a. The countries of the world know how to solve population problems.

b. There are overpopulation problems, but countries don't agree about solving them.

c. The countries of the world agree on how to create problems.

▶**EXERCISE 18** **Read the questions and answer them orally with your teacher. Then answer the questions orally with a classmate. At home, write the answers for homework. Answer in complete sentences.**

1. What continent has the most people? How many? ________________________

   ____

2. What does "global warming" mean? ________________________

   ____

3. Which three countries have 70 percent of their people below the poverty level?

   ____

4. In how many years do you think the world population is going to be seven billion?

   ____

5. What are two problems caused by overpopulation? ________________________

   ____

6. What was the United Nations conference about in South Africa in 2002? __________

   ____

7. Who keeps statistics and makes estimates? ________________________

   ____

8. What do geographers study? ________________________

   ____

Vocabulary Practice

▶EXERCISE 19 Complete the sentences with words from the box.

statistics	poverty	gases	predictions	exact
population	housing	conferences	extinct	contaminated
overpopulation	geographer			

1. The numbers that geographers keep about population are called ___________________.
2. Geographers make ___________________ about the future.
3. Some statistics are not ___________________ but only estimates.
4. Some countries are very poor, and many people live under the ___________________ level.
5. The world's ___________________ is growing faster and faster.
6. Careless government regulations add to the problem of not enough ___________________.
7. More greenhouse ___________________ affect the temperature of the earth.
8. Many plants and animals are becoming ___________________ because of overpopulation.
9. When water is polluted, it is ___________________.
10. The United Nations had two important ___________________ in 1998 and 2002.
11. A ___________________ studies the surface of the earth and its features.
12. The problem of having too many people on the earth is called ___________________.

►EXERCISE 20 Write the word from the box that means the opposite of the underlined word or words. Some words can be used more than once.

largest	least	below	most	careless
richest	disagree	decrease	polluted	enough
few	increase	contaminated		

1. China and India have the smallest populations. ____________
2. They are the most populous countries ____________
3. The water in some countries is uncontaminated. ____________
4. Some people live above the poverty level. ____________
5. The least industrialized countries produce greenhouse gases. ____________
6. Some countries have careful government regulations. ____________
7. My country produces the least greenhouse gases. ____________
8. The poorest countries are the most industrialized. ____________
9. Some countries agree about how to solve overpopulation. ____________
10. Some government regulations increase poverty. ____________
11. Uncontaminated water is clean water. ____________
12. There is insufficient food in some countries. ____________
13. There are many clean rivers. ____________
14. Countries want to decrease contamination. ____________

Expansion Activities

► **Activity 1 Vocabulary Game** *Working in groups, design and play this vocabulary game. Move from "Start" to "Finish."*

START

Contaminated

FINISH

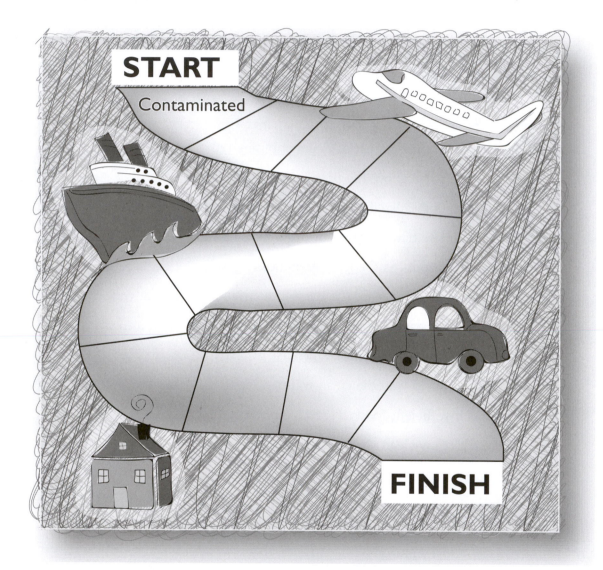

1. On a piece of paper, draw a game board like the one here.
2. Write a vocabulary word from this chapter in each square.
3. Trade your game board with another group.

4. To play, roll a die and move a marker that number of squares.
5. Give the definition for the word in the space. If your definition is correct, you can stay in the square. If not, you must return to the last space you were in.
6. The first person to reach "Finish" wins!

▸ Activity 2 Research a Country *Use the Internet or the library to find information about a country that interests you. Work in pairs or a small group and present the information that you learn to the class. Include information about topics listed below or your own ideas.*

1. location
2. population
3. size
4. languages
5. religions and ethnicities
6. important geographical features
7. interesting places to visit

Vocabulary List

Adjectives

billion
careless
contaminated
environmental
exact
extinct
incredible
industrialized
million
populous
separate
underwater

Directions

east
north
south
west

Superlatives

the biggest
the highest/lowest
the hottest/coldest
the most beautiful
the most difficult
the most incredible
the most interesting
the most populous
the poorest/richest
the smallest/largest
the tallest

Adverbs

ago
away
very
violently

Nouns

atmosphere
climate
conference
continent
detail
equator
estimate
ethnicity/ethnicities
extinction
feature
future
game
geographer
geography
geologist
global warming
greenhouse gas
habitat
heat
landmass
level
magma
mile
mountain range
ocean
overpopulation
poverty
prediction
regulation
river
statistic
surface
tectonic plate
wetland

Proper Nouns

Gondwanaland
Laurasia
Mount Everest

Continents

Africa
Antarctica
Asia
Australia
Europe
North America
South America

Languages

English
Portuguese
Spanish

Mountain Ranges

Alps
Andes
Great Dividing Range
Himalayas
Rocky Mountains

Oceans

Arctic
Atlantic
Indian
Pacific

Sea

Arabian

Verbs—Present

change
climb
increase
produce
protect
reduce
research
say
think

Verbs—Past

attended
broke
crashed
disagreed
formed
held
moved

If you want to review vocabulary and complete additional activities related to this chapter, go to the *Read to Succeed 2* Web site at http://esl.college.hmco.com/students.

CHAPTER 8

Who Were Our Ancestors?

Reading 1 Early Ancestors

Before You Read

▸EXERCISE 1 Discuss these questions with a partner or a small group.

1. How old do you think Earth is?
2. Who were our ancestors?
3. Where did our ancestors first live?

▸EXERCISE 2 Listen to your teacher read the sentences. Say the sentences after your teacher. Then match the sentences to the pictures. Write the correct letter next to the sentence.

A.

B.

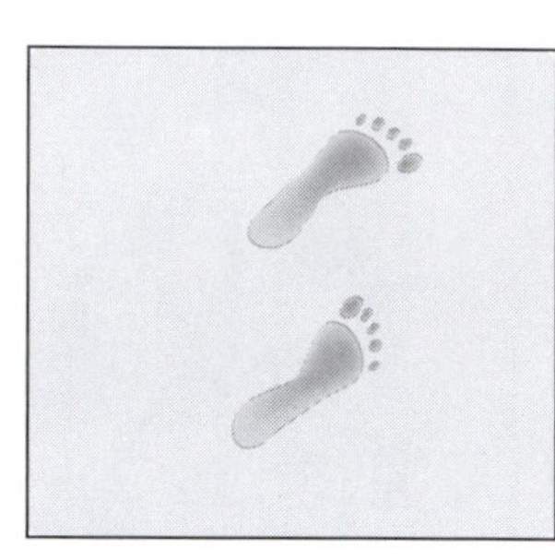

C.

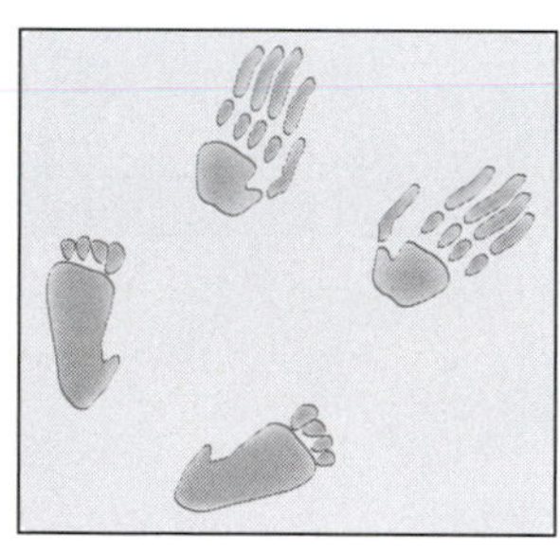

D.

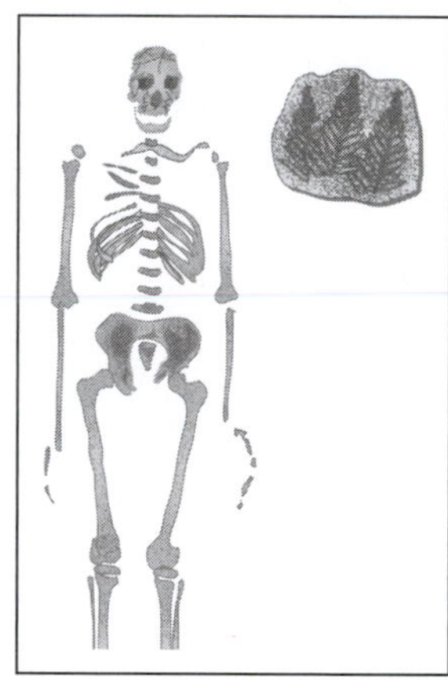

E.

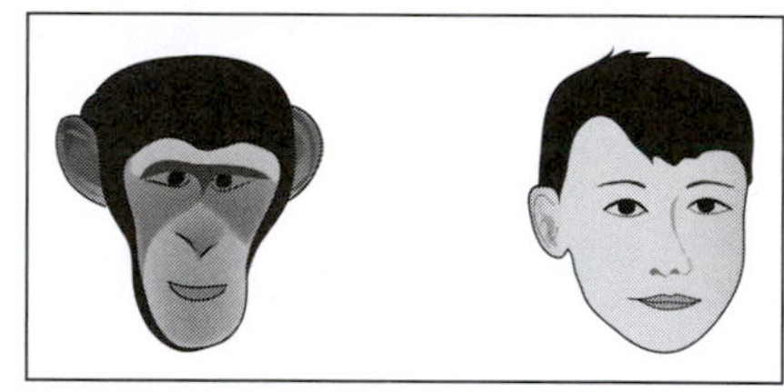

F.

1. Fossils help us learn about the past. ______
2. Human beings have their origin in Ethiopia, Africa. ______
3. Earth began billions of years ago. ______
4. Our ancestors walked on two legs. ______
5. Human beings and apes are different. ______
6. Apes do not walk on two legs. ______

▸EXERCISE 3 Circle the synonym, or similar word.

1. apes
   a. men b. monkeys c. plants
2. extinct
   a. dead b. alive c. living
3. ground
   a. stone b. soil c. wood

▸EXERCISE 4 Scan the reading and answer the questions.

1. What is a human being? ____________________
2. What are the names of some apes? ____________________
3. What changes affected animals five to six million years ago? ____________________
4. What is anthropology? ____________________
5. When did the earth form? ____________________
6. When did apes first live? ____________________
7. Where did our first ancestors live? ____________________
8. What does "homo" mean in Latin? ____________________

Words from the Reading*

ape	**extinct**	**ground**	**spine**
chimpanzee	**footprint**	**life**	

*Your teacher can help you understand these words and others listed at the end of the chapter and on the Web site at http://esl.college.hmco.com/students.

Read to learn about our early ancestors.*

Early Ancestors

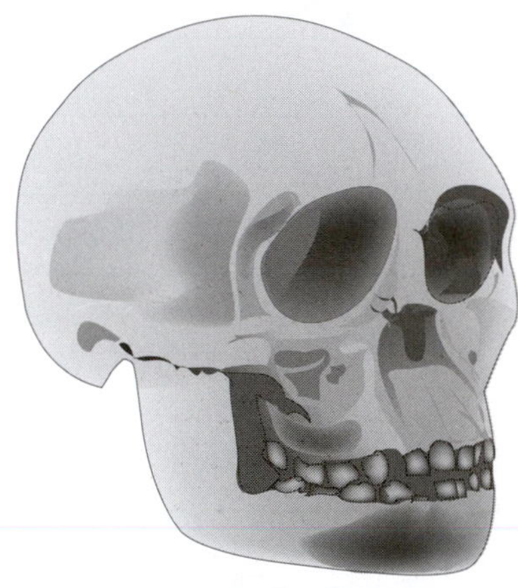
Australopithecus

Anthropologists don't know exactly when our **ancestors** lived, and there are different theories, or ideas that have no clear conclusion, about our ancestors. **Anthropology** is the study of human **origin** and culture. Anthropologists think that Earth formed five billion years ago and that life started about three billion years ago. Anthropologists say that the first animals with a spine lived 500 million years ago. We know that apes lived 33 million years ago. Apes are gorillas, chimpanzees, and other large monkeys. These apes lived in trees in Africa, had thirty-two teeth, and walked on four legs. Our ancestors also lived in Africa and had thirty-two teeth, but they were different—they walked on two legs. One theory is that our first ancestors lived three to four million years ago in Africa.

Anthropologists say that there was an ice age on Earth five to six million years ago and that the weather affected animals. The temperatures became very cold and dry, and plants and trees could not grow very well. There was a lot of ice, and the sea level **dropped.** There were not many trees, and there was a lot more grass. The apes that lived in the trees now had to walk on the ground on four legs, as they do today. Some animals became extinct and disappeared. New animals appeared on Earth over time.

Between three-and-a-half and four million years ago, a **hominid** lived that was very similar to us, Australopithecus. Human beings are part of the hominid family. This was one of our earliest ancestors. Anthropologists have his **fossils,** bones, and footprints. Our ancestors lived in the Great Rift Valley in Africa in what is now called Ethiopia. Australopithecus had a small brain, and he had thirty-two teeth like a modern **human being.** Two million years later, other human ancestors appeared on Earth, and they walked on two legs. One of these ancestors made tools from bones, stone, and wood. Anthropologists call him Homo habilis (handy man), the man who used tools. *Homo* means "man" in Latin. Anthropologists don't know exactly when our ancestors first used fire or language, but they think that these first hominids were the first human ancestors.

*Related class to take or visit: anthropology.

ancestor	a person from whom another person is descended
anthropology	the physical and cultural study of human beings
fossil	a thing left by a plant or animal that lived long ago
drop	to fall from a higher to a lower place or position
hominid	a member of the family Hominidae (humans are the only living members)
human being	a person
origin	a source or beginning

Reading Charts and Graphs

►EXERCISE 5 Study the timeline. Then answer the questions with a partner.

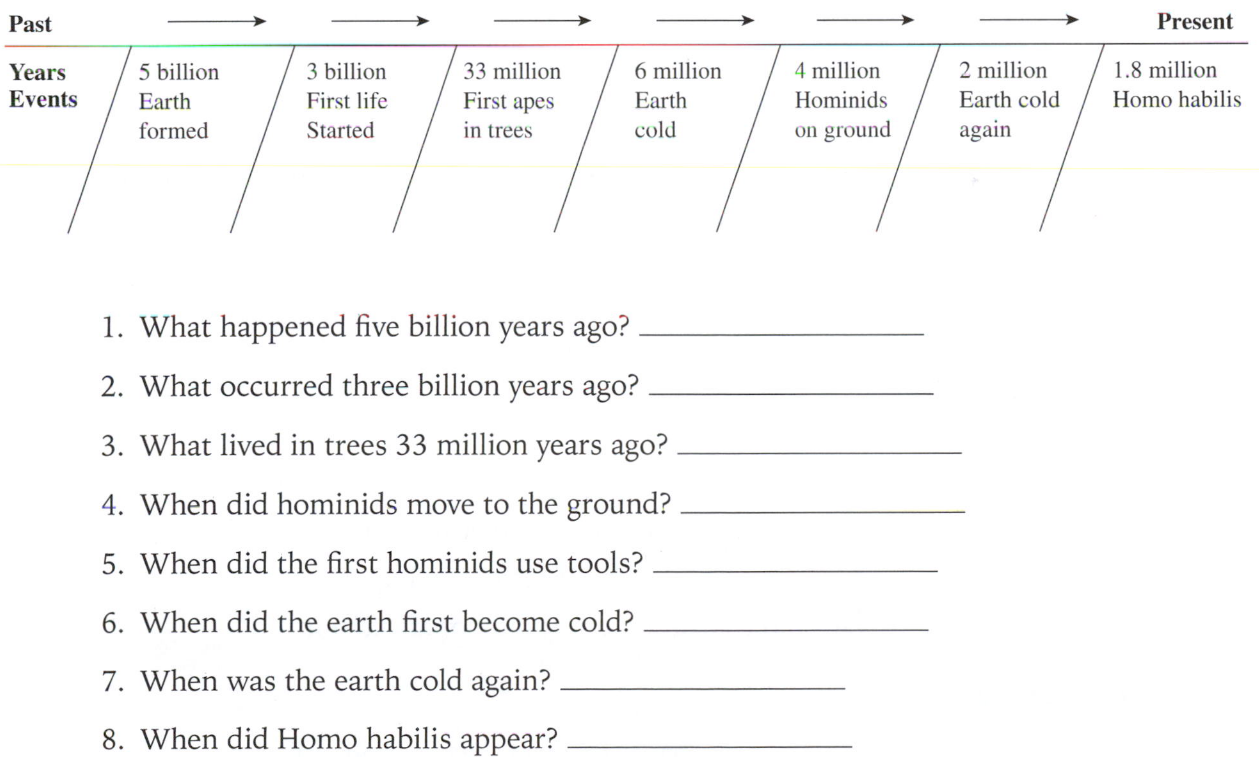

1. What happened five billion years ago? ____________________
2. What occurred three billion years ago? ____________________
3. What lived in trees 33 million years ago? ____________________
4. When did hominids move to the ground? ____________________
5. When did the first hominids use tools? ____________________
6. When did the earth first become cold? ____________________
7. When was the earth cold again? ____________________
8. When did Homo habilis appear? ____________________

Comprehension

▶EXERCISE 6. Write T (true) or F (false) for each statement.

_____ 1. Anthropology is the study of Earth's geography.

_____ 2. Earth formed five million years ago.

_____ 3. Life started five billion years ago.

_____ 4. Animals with a spine lived 500 million years ago.

_____ 5. Apes lived 33 million years ago.

_____ 6. Apes have forty-two teeth.

_____ 7. At first, apes lived on the ground.

_____ 8. Earth became warmer five to six million years ago.

_____ 9. A human being is a hominid.

_____ 10. Australopithecus had thirty-two teeth.

▶EXERCISE 7 Circle the letter of the main idea for each paragraph.

Paragraph 1:

a. The first apes walked on four legs.
b. Anthropologists know when apes lived.
c. Anthropologists don't know exactly when our ancestors lived.

Paragraph 2:

a. The weather changed on Earth five to six million years ago.
b. Five to six million years ago, the weather became very hot and wet.
c. There was a big change in the weather, but it did not affect animals.

Paragraph 3:

a. We have many fossils from apes that lived five to six million years ago.
b. Our ancestor was a hominid that lived about four million years ago.
c. Homo habilis was an ancestor of the ape.

▸EXERCISE 8 Circle the letter of the correct answer.

1. Anthropology is the study of ____________.
   a. our origin and culture b. our history c. animals
2. When did Earth form?
   a. 500 million years ago b. 33 million years ago c. 5–6 billion years ago
3. When did the first life on Earth start?
   a. 5 million years ago b. 3 billion years ago c. 33 million years ago
4. Where did the first apes live?
   a. Australia b. Africa c. the Americas
5. What big change happened five to six million years ago on Earth?
   a. The weather changed. b. Life started. c. Apes disappeared.
6. How were the temperatures during this change?
   a. warm b. cold c. the same
7. After the big change, there were ______ trees.
   a. not many b. more c. the same number of
8. What did the apes do after the big change?
   a. moved to ground b. moved to the Americas c. moved to trees
9. What became of some animals after the big change?
   a. migrated to Asia b. became extinct c. moved north
10. Apes moved to the ground ____________ because of the cold and the lack of trees.
    a. 5 billion years ago b. 1.8 million years ago c. 5 million years ago
11. On how many legs did the first apes walk? ____________
    a. four b. two c. five
12. How many teeth did our first ancestors have? ____________
    a. forty b. thirty c. thirty-two

▸EXERCISE 9 Read the questions and answer them orally with your teacher. Then answer the questions orally with a classmate. At home, write the answers for homework. Answer in complete sentences.

1. What does an anthropologist study? ______________________________

____

2. When did Earth form? ______________________________

____

3. When did the first life start? ______________________________

____

4. When did animals with a spine first live? ______________________________

____

5. What animals lived 33 million years ago? ______________________________

____

6. Where did the first apes live? Where did they live after the Ice Age? ______________

____

7. How are human beings different from apes? ______________________________

____

8. How did the temperature change on Earth six million years ago? ______________

____

Vocabulary Practice

▸EXERCISE 10 Write a synonym (or two words) from "Early Ancestors" for the underlined word or words.

1. My <u>great-great-grandparents</u> were from Haiti. ____________________ (paragraph 1)
2. <u>This science</u> studies our origin and culture. ____________________ (paragraph 1)
3. <u>Gorillas and chimpanzees</u> are intelligent. ____________________ (paragraph 1)
4. After the big change, some animals <u>died out</u>. ____________________ (paragraph 2)
5. After the big change, apes walked on <u>land</u>. ____________________ (paragraph 2)
6. Anthropologists found very <u>old bones</u> four million years old. ____________________ (paragraph 3)

7. We do not know much about our <u>distant relatives</u>. ____________________
(paragraph 3)

8. Hominids used <u>bones and stones</u> to do simple work. ____________________
(paragraph 3)

►EXERCISE 11 Make each sentence true. Write a word from the box for the <u>underlined</u> word or words.

lived	first	started	cold	disappeared
a lot of	new	many	strong	footprints

1. There was <u>a little</u> ice on the ground millions of years ago. ____________________
2. We don't know when language <u>stopped</u>. ____________________
3. Australopithecus <u>died</u> three to four million years ago. ____________________
4. Some animals <u>appeared</u> when Earth got cold. ____________________
5. The temperatures became <u>warm</u> during the ice ages. ____________________
6. The <u>last</u> animal with a spine appeared long ago. ____________________
7. There were <u>old</u> strong animals on Earth. ____________________
8. There were <u>few</u> trees before the Ice Age. ____________________
9. <u>Weak</u> animals continued to live during the Ice Age. ____________________
10. Anthropologists found our ancestors' <u>handprints</u>. ____________________

Reading 2 From Lucy to Homo Sapiens

Before You Read

►EXERCISE 12 Discuss these questions with a partner or a small group.

1. What is an ancestor?
2. Is your jaw larger or smaller than a gorilla's?
3. Do you think a human brain is larger or smaller than a chimpanzee's?

▸EXERCISE 13 Listen to your teacher read the sentences. Say the sentences after your teacher. Then match the sentences to the pictures. Write the correct letter next to the sentence.

A.

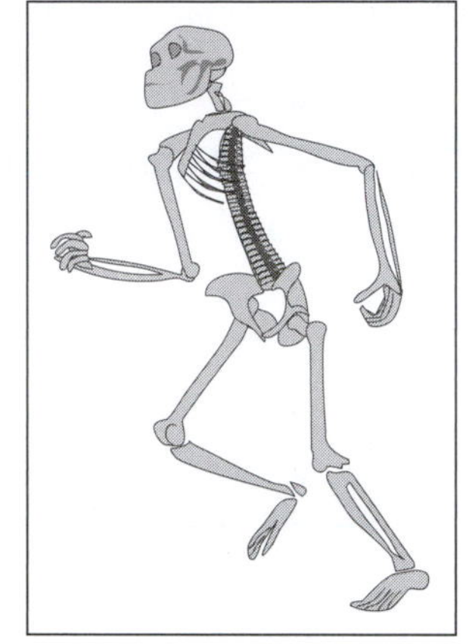

B.

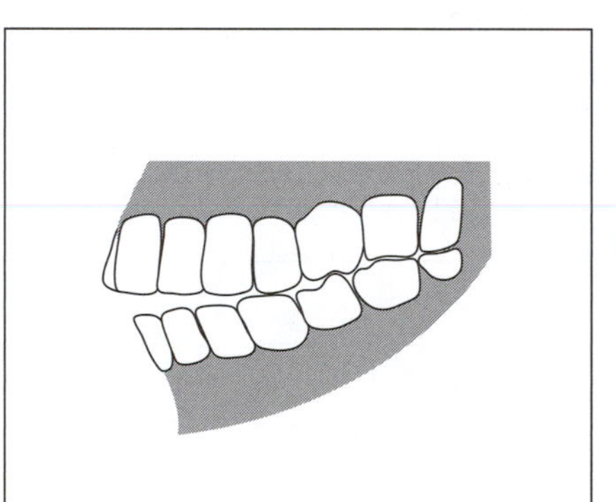

C.

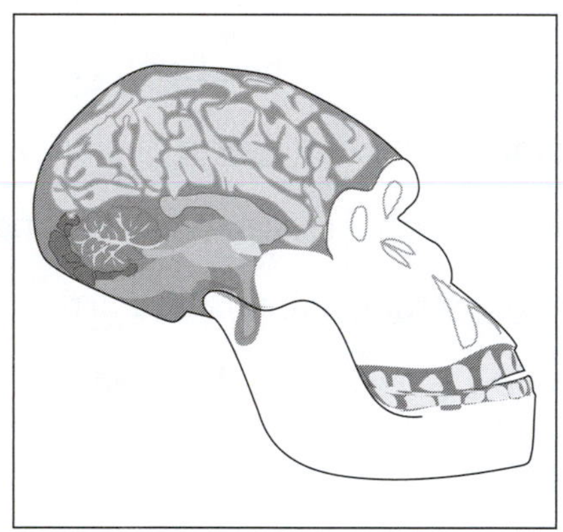

D.

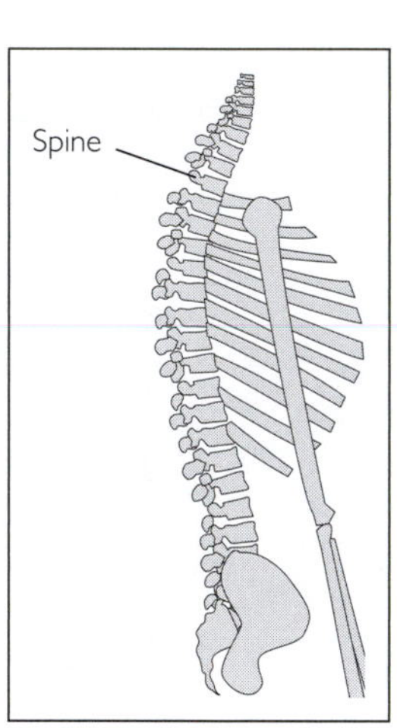

E.

1. Many animals have one in their back. ___________
2. They were on the ground five million years ago. ___________
3. Our brain is larger than the brain of early man. ___________
4. We have thirty-two in our jaw. ___________
5. Our ancestors walked on two legs. ___________

▶EXERCISE 14 Complete each sentence with a word from "Words from the Reading."

1. The continent south of Europe is ________________.
2. English and Japanese are ________________.
3. An ax and a knife are ________________.

Words from the Reading*

Africa	**Homo habilis**	**Neanderthal**
extinct	**language**	**tool**

*Your teacher can help you understand these words and others listed at the end of the chapter and on the Web site at http://esl.college.hmco.com/students.

▶EXERCISE 15 Scan the reading and answer the questions.

1. Who was Lucy? ________________________________

____
2. What happened 2.5 million years ago? ________________________________

____
3. What are Neanderthals and Homo sapiens? ________________________________

____

Read to find out about our ancestors.

From Lucy to Homo Sapiens

Anthropologists think that one of our ancestors lived three million years ago. They found her fossil bones in 1974, and they named her Lucy. She was from Ethiopia, in Africa. She walked on two legs, and she was three feet eight inches tall. She weighed only sixty-five pounds, but she was very strong. Lucy had large jaws and a large face, but she did not have a chin. She had a **brain** one-third the size of our modern brain. When she died, she was twenty-five years old. Anthropologists think that she was one of our very earliest ancestors. Lucy is important because she was a hominid, or humanlike.

Two important events took place beginning 2.5 million years ago. Another ice age happened, and two other human ancestors walked the earth. There was ice everywhere again, and, as before, the **sea level** moved down. Africa was dry again, and there were few trees. New animals appeared, and other animals became extinct and disappeared. About 1.8 million years ago, Homo habilis, or the man that used tools, appeared. Another ancestor, Homo erectus, lived 1.6 million years ago and also walked on two legs. He probably used language because of his brain size and voice box. He had a brain one-half the size of our brain. Homo erectus was also from Africa and used simple tools. Anthropologists think that he had a simple language. They think that this was our first direct ancestor, but they are not certain.

Anthropologists study two types of modern humans: Neanderthals and **Homo sapiens.** Neanderthals lived 30,000–200,000 years ago in Europe and Asia. They lived in cold climates and had a very strong body and a large nose. Neanderthals were perhaps the first to bury their dead family members and leave them offerings like flowers. Homo sapiens appeared later but were on Earth at the same time as Neanderthals. We don't know where Homo sapiens came from. They were thinner, had a larger brain, and had a flat forehead. They competed with the Neanderthals for land and food, and the Neanderthals later disappeared. Anthropologists are certain that the origin of all human beings is Africa, and they think that our ancestors moved out of Africa about 200,000 years ago. Because of recent DNA studies, anthropologists also think that all humans have a common African mother. Human beings probably had several ancestors that lived at different times.

brain	a large mass of nerve tissue enclosed in the skull; the mind
Homo sapiens	the modern species of human beings
sea level	the level of the ocean's surface

Comprehension

▶EXERCISE 16 Circle the letter of the correct answer.

1. Who lived three million years ago?

   a. our ancestor Lucy b. the first ape c. Homo sapiens

2. How do anthropologists know about Lucy?

   a. her photograph b. her body c. her bones

3. How old was Lucy when she died?

   a. 25 b. 3 million c. 18

4. How large was her brain compared to the modern human brain?

   a. the same b. one-third as large c. three-fourths as large

5. Was Lucy an ape, a hominid, or Homo habilis?

   a. Homo habilis b. ape c. hominid

6. When was there another big change on Earth?

   a. 3 million years ago b. 2.5 million years ago c. 10 million years ago

7. What became extinct again?

   a. all animals b. some animals c. Homo habilis

8. One of our direct ancestors appeared 1.8 million years ago. Who was it?
   a. Homo sapiens b. Homo habilis c. Lucy
9. What modern human lived 30 to 200,000 years ago?
   a. Homo sapiens b. Neanderthals c. Australopithecus
10. Where is the origin of all human beings?
   a. Africa b. Germany c. China

►EXERCISE 17 Circle the letter of the main idea for each paragraph.

Paragraph 1:

a. Earth is very old.
b. One of our ancestors lived three million years ago.
c. Homo habilis was strong.

Paragraph 2:

a. Homo erectus probably used language.
b. Life started 2.5 million years ago.
c. There was another ice age, and our direct ancestor lived.

Paragraph 3:

a. Neanderthals and Homo sapiens are still alive.
b. Australopithecus is a modern hominid.
c. Neanderthals and Homo sapiens are two modern humans that anthropologists study.

►EXERCISE 18 Put the information from Readings 1 and 2 in order. Number 1 is the oldest event, and number 10 is the most recent.

a. Hominids moved to the ground. ______
b. Earth became cold for the first time. ______
c. Homo habilis appeared 1.8 million years ago. ______
d. The first life started three billion years ago. ______
e. The first apes lived in trees 33 million years ago. ______
f. Earth formed 5–6 billion years ago. __*1*__
g. Earth became cold again 2.5 million years ago. ______
h. Lucy lived 3 million years ago. ______
i. Neanderthals appeared 200,000 years ago. ______
j. Homo sapiens appeared. __*10*__

▸EXERCISE 19 Read the questions and answer them orally with your teacher. Then answer the questions orally with a classmate. At home, write the answers for homework. Answer in complete sentences.

1. Who lived in Ethiopia, Africa, 3 million years ago? ______________________

____

2. How tall was she, and how much did she weigh? ______________________

____

3. How large was her brain? ______________________

____

4. What change happened on Earth 2.5 million years ago? ______________________

____

5. Who lived 1.8 million years ago? ______________________

____

6. What did he use with his hands? ______________________

____

7. Did Homo habilis appear before or after Lucy? ______________________

____

8. What continent was Homo habilis from? ______________________

____

9. What two modern ancestors are related to modern human beings? ______________________

____

10. How many ancestors do modern humans have? ______________________

____

11. When did our ancestors move out of Africa? ______________________

____

12. Who has a common African mother? ______________________

____

Vocabulary Practice

▶**EXERCISE 20 Read the following words. What categories can they be divided into? Write the name of a category next to each number. Then write the words under the correct category.**

Ethiopia	bones	Africa	Asia	face
legs	ancestors	Homo habilis	body	Europe
nose	Homo erectus	forehead	Homo sapiens	brain
Neanderthals	jaws	Australopithecus	Lucy	

1. *hominids*	2. ________	3. ________
Homo erectus	________	________
________	________	________
________	________	________
________	________	________
________	________	________
________	________	________
________	________	________
________	________	________

▶**EXERCISE 21 Write a word found in "From Lucy to Homo Sapiens" that completes each sentence.**

1. The important organ inside our head is the ________________.
2. Modern human beings are called ________________.
3. The level of the ocean is called ________________.
4. Human beings have a ________________ in their back.
5. The place of origin of all humans and their ancestors was ________________.
6. Our ancestor who used tools was ________________.
7. The first people to bury their dead were ________________.
8. When Earth became very cold, this was called an ________________.

Expansion Activities

►Activity 1 A Letter from Homo Habilis *Write a letter to your teacher as if you were Homo habilis. Include a description of the changes on Earth because of the Ice Age and information about yourself, your family, and your life. You may need to do an Internet search to find more information about Homo habilis. Use the keywords* Homo habilis, early man, anthropology, *or* human ancestors.

►Activity 2 Crossword Puzzle *Complete the puzzle using the clues provided.*

1 2 3 4 5 6 7 8 9 10 11

Ancestor Puzzle

Across

2. A synonym for *the same as*.
4. Lucy had a large ______.
5. Homo habilis used simple ______.
6. The country where Lucy was found.
8. Lucy did not have one.
9. The antonym for *weak*.
10. Anthrolopogists have Lucy's ______.
11. Homo habilis's ______ was one-half of ours.

Down

1. Anthropologists study our ______.
3. She lived three million years ago.
4. A plant or animal that lived long ago.
6. Animals that disappeared are ______.
7. Your great-great-grandparents.

Vocabulary List

Adjectives
certain
direct
dry
early
extinct
flat
more
similar
simple
small
strong
thinner

Adverbs
again
down
everywhere
later
perhaps

Nouns
Africa
ancestor
anthropology
ape
bone
brain
change
chimpanzee
chin
Ethiopia
event
footprint
forehead
fossil
gorilla
grass
ground
hominid
Homo
Homo habilis
Homo sapiens
human being
jaw
language
Latin
leg
life
Neanderthal
offering
pound
sea level
spine
tool
tooth/teeth
tree
type
voice box

Verbs—Present
bury
grow
leave

Verbs—Past
affected
appeared
became
called
disappeared
dropped
found
made
started
used
walked
was/were
weighed

If you want to review vocabulary and complete additional activities related to this chapter, go to the *Read to Succeed 2* Web site at http://esl.college.hmco.com/students.

UNIT 3

Readings in Science and Technology

CHAPTER 9

You Can't Control Mother Nature

Reading 1 Natural Disasters

Before You Read

▶**EXERCISE 1 Discuss these questions with a partner or a small group.**

1. What do you think "Mother Nature" means?
2. Are there any earthquakes, hurricanes, or tornadoes where you live?
3. What happens in an earthquake?
4. What kind of storm produces a funnel-shaped cloud?

▶**EXERCISE 2 Listen to your teacher read the sentences. Say the sentences after your teacher. Then match the sentences to the pictures. Write the correct letter next to the sentence.**

A.

B.

C.

D.

E.

F.

1. A tornado is a circular funnel cloud from the sky that touches the ground. ______
2. A tornado can destroy houses and buildings. ______
3. Sometimes buildings burn after an earthquake. ______
4. A hurricane has strong winds and heavy rain. ______
5. After a hurricane, large areas are flooded. ______
6. When an earthquake occurs, everything moves suddenly. ______

▶**EXERCISE 3 Draw a line to match the two parts of each sentence.**

1. A hurricane is	a. the ground shakes and buildings fall.
2. A tornado is in the shape of	b. a funnel-shaped cloud.
3. In an earthquake,	c. strong circular wind, rain, and flooding.

Words from the Reading*

building	shaped
disaster	sky
flooding	storm
funnel	wind

*Your teacher can help you understand these words and others listed at the end of the chapter and on the Web site at http://esl.college.hmco.com/students.

▶**EXERCISE 4 Scan the reading and answer the questions.**

1. What natural disasters is this essay about? ______________________________

____

2. How do people feel after a natural disaster? ______________________________

____

3. How well do you think we can plan before a natural disaster? ________________

____

Read to learn about disasters that occur in nature.

Natural Disasters

Many natural disasters occur every year, and sometimes we can prepare for them. Earthquakes, hurricanes, and tornadoes occur all over the world. They cause deaths as well as heavy damage to homes and businesses. They cost families, insurance companies, and cities billions of dollars in rebuilding costs.

A **hurricane** always starts as a tropical storm in the ocean. It produces very fast **circular** winds on land that cause damage to buildings and bring high ocean waves that cause flooding. Hurricanes are rated from category 1 to 5 (winds from 74 to 155 miles per hour).* The high winds bring in great amounts of water. Hurricane Isabel struck the southeastern United States in September 2003. Like many hurricanes, Isabel started in the Atlantic Ocean and then moved steadily toward land until it hit the coast of North Carolina. Hurricane Isabel lasted 3 days and left 40 people dead, 600,000 buildings destroyed or damaged, heavy flooding, and 2 million people without electricity! Scientists predicted when the hurricane would hit land and warned people. Many people evacuated, but others refused to leave. The cost of the hurricane was billions of dollars.

*National Hurricane Center.

Earthquakes can happen anywhere on the earth without warning because scientists can't predict earthquakes yet. An **earthquake** happens when heat and pressure inside the earth build up and crack the earth's crust. Countries along the Pacific Ocean, or Ring of Fire, have the most earthquakes. One of the biggest and most deadly recent earthquakes happened in the early morning on September 19, 1985, in Mexico City. Suddenly, everything began moving, and many buildings fell. During the three-minute earthquake, people hid or ran from their apartments, but 10,000 people died! This powerful earthquake measured 8.1 out of a possible 10 on the **Richter Scale.** After the earthquake, people felt nervous, helpless, and afraid, and all emergency services were very busy. One hundred thousand people lost their homes or apartments, and about seven thousand buildings in the city fell or were damaged. There was a lot of destruction, and many people were unprepared.

Hundreds of tornadoes occur every year in the United States, and they destroy many buildings and homes. Several very strong tornadoes hit Florida in 1998, picking up cars and houses. When tornadoes form, warm, moist air from the Gulf of Mexico moves north and meets cold Canadian air. This air moves into what is called Tornado Alley, in the states of Texas, Oklahoma, Kansas, and Nebraska.** A **tornado** is a terrible and dangerous **spinning** storm. It produces a funnel-shaped cloud that comes down from the sky and touches the land, destroying everything it touches. A tornado lasts ten minutes to an hour but produces winds that are even stronger than a hurricane's winds.** A tornado can lift the roofs off houses, lift cars and trailers, and turn houses into matchsticks. One positive thing about tornadoes is that there is a tornado warning system so that people can leave or take cover to protect themselves.

**U.S. National Weather Service.

circular	shaped like a circle
earthquake	a sudden, violent movement of Earth's surface
hurricane	a severe tropical storm with heavy rains and winds exceeding 74 miles per hour
Richter Scale	a scale used to express the size or total energy of an earthquake from 1 to 10
spinning	turning rapidly
tornado	a violent, circular windstorm in the form of a column of air several hundred yards wide

Comprehension

▶EXERCISE 5 Write T (true) or F (false) for each statement.

_____ 1. Natural disasters occur every five years.

_____ 2. There is no early hurricane warning system.

_____ 3. A hurricane is a funnel-shaped storm.

_____ 4. Hurricanes cause floods when they hit the ocean.

_____ 5. Earthquakes can occur anywhere on the earth.

_____ 6. Scientists can predict an earthquake and warn us.

_____ 7. The Mexico City hurricane was very strong.

_____ 8. Ten thousand people died in the Florida tornado.

_____ 9. During a tornado, the ground starts moving.

_____ 10. A tornado produces a funnel-shaped cloud.

▶EXERCISE 6 Circle the letter of the main idea for each paragraph.

Paragraph 1:

a. Earthquakes, tornadoes, and hurricanes are rated from 1 to 10.
b. Natural disasters occur every year, but we can often prepare for them.
c. Natural disasters occur every year in the ocean.

Paragraph 2:

a. Hurricanes are rated from 1 to 5.
b. A hurricane is a tropical storm that causes damage on land.
c. Hurricane Isabel's funnel cloud destroyed buildings.

Paragraph 3:

a. Earthquakes happen anywhere, but we can predict them.
b. Earthquakes occur suddenly anywhere on the earth.
c. We measure earthquakes with the Richter Scale.

Paragraph 4:

a. Tornado Alley is on the East Coast.
b. A tornado's winds are stronger than a hurricane's winds.
c. Tornadoes occur frequently in the United States and are dangerous.

▸EXERCISE 7 Match the two parts of each sentence.

1. Natural disasters ______
2. Hurricanes always start ______
3. Hurricanes begin as ______
4. Hurricane Isabel caused ______
5. After an earthquake, ______
6. A powerful earthquake is ______
7. Scientists can predict ______
8. Tornadoes can pick up ______
9. The funnel-shaped cloud is a ______
10. Families can prepare for ______
11. Hurricanes are rated ______
12. The Ring of Fire is ______
13. The Richter Scale ______
14. A tornado is ______

a. tropical storms.
b. emergency services are busy.
c. 8.0 or more on the Richter Scale.
d. hurricanes and tornadoes.
e. cars and houses.
f. tornado.
g. some natural disasters.
h. floods and heavy damage.
i. in the ocean.
j. occur every year.
k. measures earthquakes.
l. a spinning storm.
m. from 1 to 5.
n. along the Pacific Ocean.

▸EXERCISE 8 Read the questions, and answer them orally with your teacher. Then answer the questions orally with a classmate. At home, write the answers for homework. Answer in complete sentences.

About the Reading

1. What are three examples of natural disasters? ______________________

   ____

2. Where did Hurricane Isabel occur and when? ______________________

   ____

3. What happened when Isabel moved onto land? ______________________

   ____

4. What do the high winds cause during a hurricane? ______________________

   ____

5. Where is the Ring of Fire, and what happens there? ______________________

   ____

6. Do we know when the next earthquake will happen? Why? ______________________

   ____

7. Where is Tornado Alley? ______________________

   ____

8. What does a tornado look like, and what does it do? ______________________

   ____

About You

9. Are there natural disasters where you live? ______________________

   ____

10. Does your family have a plan for a natural disaster? ______________________

    ____

11. Were you in a natural disaster once?

    ____

12. Are there other natural disasters where you live now?

    ____

Vocabulary Practice

▶EXERCISE 9 Complete each sentence with a word from the box.

buildings	winds	storm	funnel	damage
circular	earthquakes	hurricane	tornadoes	deaths
evacuated	destroyed			

1. The cloud from a tornado looks like a ____________________.
2. Many ____________________ fall or are damaged after a strong earthquake.
3. A hurricane produces heavy flooding and very strong ____________________.
4. Most hurricanes begin in the ocean as a tropical ____________________.
5. There were forty ____________________ during Hurricane Isabel in September 2003.
6. A strong hurricane causes ____________________ to houses and buildings.
7. A tornado produces very strong ____________________ winds in a funnel-shaped cloud.
8. People think ____________________ happen only near the Pacific Ocean, but they don't.
9. There is an early alert or warning system for a ____________________.
10. Scientists can warn people when ____________________ are coming.
11. Many building are ____________________ during natural disasters.
12. Many houses were empty after Hurricane Isabel because people ____________________ them.

▶EXERCISE 10 Complete each sentence with a geographical word or words from the box.

Gulf of Mexico	Tornado Alley	Mexico City	Ring of Fire
Atlantic Ocean	North Carolina	Earth	Nebraska
world	Canadian		

1. ________________ is one of the states in Tornado Alley.
2. Tornadoes frequently begin in the ________________.
3. The area in the Pacific Ocean where many earthquakes occur is the ________________.
4. Many hurricanes in the United States start in the ________________.
5. Ten thousand people died in the ________________ earthquake.
6. Hurricane Isabel first hit the state of ________________.
7. Natural disasters can take place anywhere on ________________.
8. Texas, Oklahoma, and Kansas are part of ________________.
9. Natural disasters occur each year in the ________________.
10. Tornadoes form when warm air from the Gulf of Mexico meets cold ________________ air.

▶EXERCISE 11 Read the explanation. Write the <u>underlined</u> word with the prefix indicated.

Prefixes are letters at the beginning of a word that change the meaning of the word.

Prefix	**New Word**
re- (again) *This food is cold. I have to <u>heat</u> it again.*	reheat
pre- (before) *We had to <u>cut</u> the wood before we rebuilt the house.*	precut
un- (not) *Some buildings were not <u>damaged</u>.*	undamaged

1. *re-* Please <u>tell</u> your story again to the police. retell
2. *re-* The people need to <u>build</u> their homes again. ____________
3. un- Many people were not prepared for the disaster. ____________
4. *re-* Some people <u>moved</u> their family before the tornado. ____________
5. *pre-* We had to <u>warm</u> our food before we ate it. ____________
6. *un-* We need fresh food that is not <u>cooked</u>. ____________
7. *un-* Luckily, many people were not <u>hurt</u>. ____________
8. *re-* The car stopped. We had to <u>start</u> it. ____________
9. *un-* Many areas were not <u>affected</u> by the earthquake. ____________
10. *re-* After the disaster, some people <u>appeared</u> at their homes again. ____________
11. *un-* Emergency services were not <u>available</u> after the tornado. ____________

Reading 2 Understanding and Preparing for Natural Disasters

Before You Read

▸EXERCISE 12 Discuss these questions with a partner or a small group.

1. Why is it important to prepare for an earthquake, hurricane, or tornado?
2. Does a family need a plan to prepare for an emergency or natural disaster?
3. What supplies are important after a natural disaster?

▶EXERCISE 13 **Listen to your teacher read the sentences. Say the sentences after your teacher. Then match the sentences to the pictures. Write the correct letter next to the sentence.**

A.

B.

C.

D.

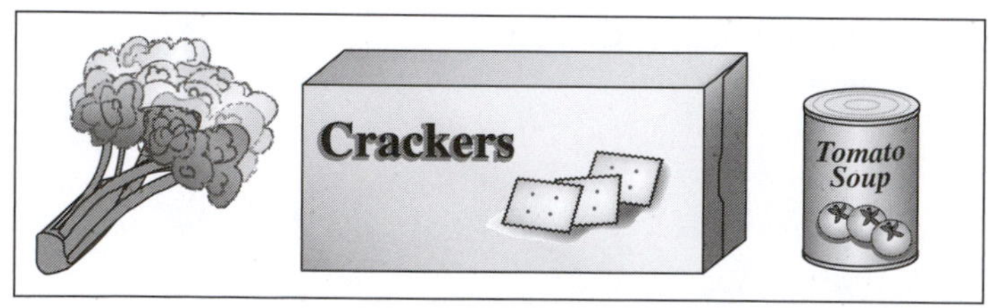

E.

F.

1. These supplies are important if there is a natural disaster or accident. ______
2. If there is a disaster, we need to eat our food in this order. ______
3. We need five gallons per person per week. ______
4. A cellar is safe if there is a tornado. ______
5. During an earthquake, a car or truck is very strong. ______
6. We can protect windows with wooden panels. ______

▸EXERCISE 14 Circle True (T) or False (F).

1. A scientist who studies earthquakes is a geologist. T F
2. A scientist who studies hurricanes is a meteorologist. T F
3. A tornado watcher causes tornadoes. T F

▸EXERCISE 15 Scan the reading and answer the questions.

1. For what natural disaster is there no warning? ______

______
2. When do hurricanes usually happen? ______

______
3. Where is the safest place during a tornado? ______

______
4. How many earthquakes are there each year? ______

______
5. What can happen after an earthquake? ______

______
6. For what two natural disasters are there warnings? ______

______
7. In your opinion which of the three natural disasters is the most dangerous? ______

______

Words from the Reading*

geologist **tornado watcher**
meteorologist

*Your teacher can help you understand these words and others listed at the end of the chapter and on the Web site at http://esl.college.hmco.com/students.

Read to find out about how we can prepare for natural disasters.

Understanding and Preparing for Natural Disasters

Scientists can give warnings for hurricanes and tornadoes but not for earthquakes; however, people can prepare for natural disasters. After a natural disaster occurs, there are usually no services for days. Emergency services, gas and electric companies, telephones, and supermarkets are very busy. It is important for families to have a plan to be independent of services for a few days. There are some important **steps** for you and your family to take before, during, and after a disaster.

We know that hurricanes usually happen in the eastern United States between June and November. Meteorologists give hurricane watches and warnings, and tell people where the hurricane is expected. This huge storm causes very strong winds, heavy tropical rain, and dangerous flooding that can last up to a week. Along the coast, the water level can rise up to eighteen feet above normal! We can prepare by **evacuating** when we hear a hurricane warning, which means the hurricane is expected within twenty-four hours.* If we stay in our house, we should hide in the middle of the house, away from windows. It is important to cover the windows with strong wooden panels. Families also have to protect their pets or farm animals, or take them to a shelter. Emergency **supplies** such as water, food, medicines, a flashlight, and a portable radio are necessary.

A tornado, or twister, brings a dangerous funnel cloud from the sky and destroys what it touches on land. Tornadoes usually occur in the Midwest and along the eastern United States in spring or early summer. Many tornadoes can form at the same time, and there are hundreds of tornadoes in one year in the United States.** A tornado can sometimes destroy all the houses on one street, but not touch houses on the next street! People who try to chase a tornado are called tornado watchers. First, people are told on radio or television that there is a tornado **watch**, then a tornado **warning.** A family must move to the safest place possible after they hear a tornado warning.** The safest place during a tornado is the basement of a strong house or the middle of a house under a strong table or in a doorway. The best place to hide outside is to lie flat in a **ditch.** After a tornado, emergency supplies are also necessary until emergency services are available again.

*U.S. National Hurricane Center.
**U.S. National Weather Service.

Geologists say there are one million earthquakes on the earth each year, so it is important to plan. Between September and October of 2003, there were five earthquakes in the world measuring 6.5 to 8.3 on the Richter Scale!*** Geologists cannot predict earthquakes. A very active earthquake zone is the San Andreas Fault, which runs between San Francisco and northern Mexico. Some geologists think a large earthquake will happen in California before 2032.*** It is important to plan and prepare now because sometimes a family is not together during and after an earthquake. The parents are at work, and the children are at school. After a large earthquake, emergency services can be **overwhelmed.** It is important to have water, **nonperishable** food, a first-aid kit, a portable radio, and a wrench to turn off the gas if necessary.

Officials and scientists can predict some natural disasters but not others. It is important to have a plan and necessary supplies for the family to survive after the disaster.

***U.S. Geological Survey.

ditch	a long, narrow trench dug in the ground
evacuating	leaving in a hurry
nonperishable	not likely to decay or spoil easily
overwhelmed	completely overpowered
step	an action taken
supply	material stored and given out when needed
warning	a sign, indication, notice, or threat of coming danger
watch	close observation

Comprehension

▶EXERCISE 16 Write T (true) or F (false) for each statement.

______ 1. Scientists often give earthquake warnings.

______ 2. Meteorologists can predict earthquakes.

______ 3. Meteorologists give hurricane watches and warnings.

______ 4. Tornadoes cause the water level to rise eighteen feet.

______ 5. There are hundreds of tornadoes in the United States each year.

______ 6. A safe place during a tornado is the basement of a house.

______ 7. Geologists can't predict earthquakes yet.

______ 8. A large earthquake could happen in California before 2032.

______ 9. The San Andreas Fault is an active earthquake zone.

______ 10. Families should have a plan and supplies for natural disasters.

▸EXERCISE 17 Complete the main idea for each paragraph.

Paragraph 1:

There are warnings ____________________.

Paragraph 2:

____________________ between June and November.

Paragraph 3:

____________________ funnel cloud ____________________.

Paragraph 4:

Geologists say ____________________.

▸EXERCISE 18 Read the questions and answer them orally with your teacher. Then answer the questions orally with a classmate. At home, write the answers for homework. Answer in complete sentences.

1. What happens to emergency services after natural disasters? ____________________
____
2. Where and when do hurricanes usually take place in the United States? ____________
____
3. What does a meteorologist study? ____________________________
____
4. What are watches and warnings? ____________________________
____
5. What does a geologist study? ____________________________
____
6. When is California likely to have a large earthquake? ____________________
____
7. Why is an emergency plan important for families? ____________________
____
8. What emergency supplies do we need for a natural disaster? ________________
____

9. What do some geologists predict will happen in 2032? ______

______

10. What are some examples of nonperishable food? ______

______

Vocabulary Practice

▶EXERCISE 19 Write a synonym for each underlined word or words. Choose from words from "Understanding and Preparing for Natural Disasters."

Paragraph 1

1. There were numerous hurricane notices before the hurricane. ______
2. We need to be able to be alone after an earthquake. ______
3. People can take important actions to prepare for a tornado. ______

Paragraph 2

4. The radio announced when the tornado is coming. ______
5. The water can go up many feet during a hurricane. ______
6. My neighbors were leaving before the tornado. ______

Paragraph 3

7. Our room below the ground is the safest room to hide during a tornado.

   ______

8. A hole in the ground is also a good place to hide. ______

Paragraph 4

9. It's important to decide what to do in case of a natural disaster.

   ______

10. Food that does not go bad or spoil is important for disasters. ______

▸EXERCISE 20 Complete each sentence with a word from the box.

step	supplies	warning	geologist	meteorologist
evacuate	destroy	form	predict	touch
twister	watchers	occur	watches	

1. The funnel cloud can ________________ the ground and destroy houses.
2. My sister studies the weather. She is a ________________.
3. Having nonperishable food is one ________________ we can take before a disaster.
4. Emergency ________________ are necessary before a tornado.
5. The police told us to ________________ before the hurricane hit our town.
6. A ________________ studies the earth and earthquakes.
7. Geologists can't ________________ earthquakes yet.
8. We left our home after we heard the hurricane ________________ on the radio.
9. Tornadoes ________________ some houses but leave other houses standing.
10. Many tornadoes can ________________ at the same time.
11. A natural disaster can ________________ at any time.
12. Tornado ________________ go, drive, or chase after tornadoes.
13. A tornado is the same as a ________________.
14. Hurricane ________________ are not as serious as hurricane warnings.

Reading Charts and Graphs

▸**EXERCISE 21** **Study the charts. Then answer the questions.**

Emergency Supplies and Planning Needed *Before* an Earthquake, Tornado, or Hurricane

Tell the Family:

How to turn off the gas and electricity
Where to hide
Where to meet after the disaster

It Is Necessary to Put:

Heavy things on the floor
Flammable and dangerous liquids outside
For hurricanes, wood panels on windows

It Is Important to Have:

Picnic supplies
Five gallons of water per person per week
A portable radio and a first-aid kit
Nonperishable food for 5 days
Personal articles and medicines
A flashlight and batteries
A wrench to turn off the gas
An earthquake or evacuation plan
A water heater secured to the wall

1. It is important to tell the family ____________________.
2. We need 5 gallons of water ____________________.
3. We should put flammable liquids ____________________.
4. You can use a ____________________ to turn off the gas.

What to Do *During* an Earthquake, Tornado, or Hurricane

Inside a House or Building:	Outside a House or Building:
Hide in a strong room or under a table	Get away from falling buildings
Hide in the basement if possible	Be careful of fallen electrical lines
Get away from windows and glass	Sit in your car or truck
Protect the family from falling objects	Listen to emergency information

5. If you are inside during an earthquake, a good place to hide is a ____________________.
6. During a tornado, a ____________________ is a good place to hide.
7. Always ____________________ from windows and glass during a natural disaster.
8. If you are outside during an earthquake, ____________________ are dangerous.

After an Earthquake, Tornado, or Hurricane

It Is Important to:	Dangers:
Turn off the gas if you smell gas	Buildings and houses falling
Turn off electricity and water	Fires from gas and electricity
Check the house for glass or fires	Landslides or flooding
Check for flammable liquids	High sea waves on the coast

9. If you smell ________________ after an earthquake, turn it ________________.

10. After a large tornado, turn off ________________.

11. Sometimes after tornadoes and earthquakes, there are ________________.

12. Two things that hurricanes produce are ________________ and ________________.

Expansion Activities

▸Activity 1 Write a Story *Have you ever been in an emergency or a disaster? Write a short story about a personal emergency or disaster that you or someone you know has experienced. In your story, tell what the disaster was, where you were, how you felt, and how you reacted.*

▸Activity 2 Natural Disaster Preparation *Do the following activities with your family or the people you live with to prepare for a natural disaster.*

A. Put each person's name on the card, and mark Yes or No for each person. Create other cards with different emergency plans.

Name	Can turn off gas and electricity	Can call 911	Knows where to meet after disaster	Has 5 gallons of water

B. Write the emergency supplies that you have and that you need to buy. Use the information in "Understanding and Preparing for Natural Disasters" to help you.

I have ___________________________

____

____

I need to buy

____

____

____

C. Is your house ready? Write what you already prepared in your house and what you still need to do. Use the information in "Understanding and Preparing for Natural Disasters" to help you.

I already ___________________________

____

____

I still need

____

____

Vocabulary List

Adjectives
active
available
circular
damaged
deadly
destroyed
each
emergency
flammable
heavy
natural
nonperishable
overwhelmed
portable
spinning
sudden
ten
tropical

Adverbs
inside
outside
suddenly
together
yet

Nouns
alert
basement
building
coast
damage
disaster
ditch
earthquake
electricity
evacuation
fault
fire
first-aid kit
flashlight
flood
flooding
floor
funnel
geologist
hurricane
land
landslide
liquid
meteorologist
Richter Scale
Ring of Fire
sea wave
sky/skies
step
storm
supply/supplies
tornado
tornado watcher
warning
watch
water heater
wrench
Services
911
electric company
gas company
police

Verbs—Present
bring
cause
destroy
evacuate
expect
fall
happen
hide
hit
measure
occur
predict
run
touch
turn off

Verbs—Past
died
evacuated
fell
hid
lasted
predicted
ran
refused
shaped
struck
warned

If you want to review vocabulary and complete additional activities related to this chapter, go to the *Read to Succeed 2* Web site at http://esl.college.hmco.com/students.

CHAPTER 10

Sharing or Stealing Music?

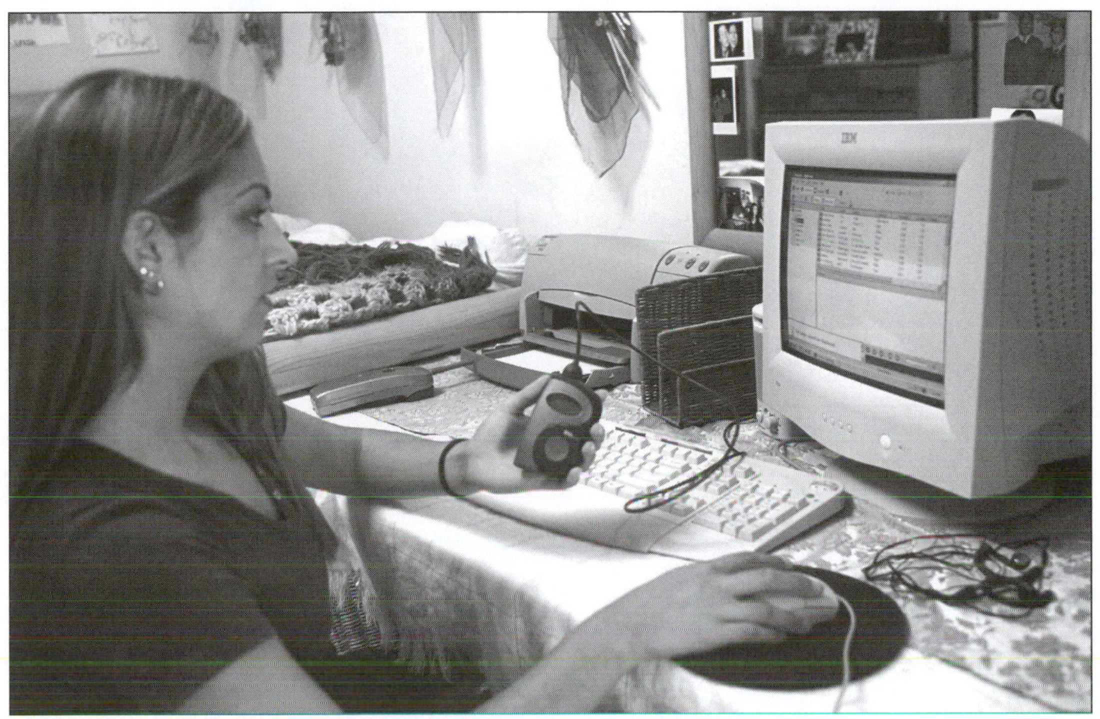

Reading 1 Sharing Music with Friends

Before You Read

▸EXERCISE 1 Discuss these questions with a partner or a small group.

1. What kind of music do you listen to?
2. Do you buy music CDs? Do you think the price of CDs is too high?
3. Do you know people who copy music on a computer free over the Internet?

▸EXERCISE 2 Listen to your teacher read the sentences. Say the sentences after your teacher. Then match the sentences to the pictures. Write the correct letter next to the sentence.

A.

B.

C.

D.

E.

F.

1. The music industry took people to court and sued them for $150,000 per shared song! ______
2. People download free music from the Internet, then record it on blank (new or empty) CDs. ______
3. Brenda downloads (copies) free music from the Internet every week and shares it with other people. ______
4. The prices of CDs are too high for many people. ______
5. File-sharing services allow people to download music free over the Internet. ______
6. The music industry considers a person who downloads music free from the Internet a thief, just as a person who steals CDs from a store is considered to be a thief. ______

▸EXERCISE 3 Circle True (T) or False (F).

1. If you break the law, you do something illegal.	T	F
2. To share is to use or enjoy with another person.	T	F
3. To sue another person is to take him or her to court.	T	F
4. A robber is the same as a thief.	T	F
5. There is competition among record companies.	T	F
6. The opposite of breaking the law is obeying the law.	T	F

▸EXERCISE 4 Scan the reading; then complete the main idea.

Paragraph 1: Young people like music, but ______________________.

Paragraph 2: Uploaders don't feel they ______________________.

Paragraph 3: The RIAA decided to sue ______________________.

Words from the Reading*

break the law **sue**
competition **thief**
share

*Your teacher can help you understand these words and others listed at the end of the chapter and on the Web site at http://esl.college.hmco.com/students.

Read to find out about downloading and sharing music for free.

Sharing Music with Friends

Brenda loves to listen to music like most young people, but she can't afford the high CD prices that record companies charge for popular CDs. She is a nineteen-year-old full-time college student, and she earns money from her low salary and good tips working as a waitress part time. She rents an apartment with three other roommates, she pays her own tuition, and she also pays most of her personal expenses. Her solution to expensive CDs is to **download** or copy music from the Internet. Brenda and millions of other people are called "downloaders" because they download free file-sharing software and music. The **file-sharing** services or sites upload the files on the Internet and offer them free to others. When Brenda later gives, shares, or trades her music files free over the Internet, she is also an **uploader.** She considers herself an active music uploader; the music industry considers her a thief.

Brenda and other uploaders do not feel that they are doing anything **illegal** or breaking the law since they are only sharing music files with others. She really enjoys the music she downloads, and she thinks using the computer to do it is fun. She says that she is not selling the songs or buying them. Brenda says that the prices of CDs are ridiculously high at $17 to $20 each, and there are only two or three good songs on each CD. The file-sharing program service is free to her on the Internet. Brenda downloads only the songs that she likes and then uploads them to share with other people. She can also burn or record the music on blank CDs and add them to her collection. Last year, she downloaded hundreds of songs and recorded them on CDs! Brenda thinks the record companies decided to get strict recently only because CD **profits** were down and competition from other companies was up. Brenda and the sixty million others who do the same all over the world now might have a legal problem because of recent lawsuits by the **recording industry.**

From 2001 to 2003, the Recording Industry Association of America (RIAA) sued and fined file-sharing services, for uploading music files, and people, for breaking the law by downloading music. In 2001, recording companies filed lawsuits against file-sharing services such as KaZaA and Napster, and also against individuals. Napster was shut down by the lawsuit. The record labels wanted fines of $150,000 for every traded or shared song. A *fine* is money you pay for doing something wrong. In early 2003, RIAA sued a twelve-year-old girl from New York who downloaded music from the Internet, and her mother had to pay a $2,000 fine. The young girl said she did not know it was illegal since anyone can use the Internet. The RIAA also sued a sixty-six-year-old grandmother from Boston, Massachusetts, for sharing more than 2,000 songs, and the RIAA wanted to charge her $150,000 per song! In the fall of 2003, the RIAA also filed lawsuits against 261 other people because they **swapped** songs. Some people ask if suing your future customers is really good business for music companies.

It is very clear that downloading and uploading free music from the Internet is not something the entertainment industry agrees with. It is sharing for the uploaders, but it is stealing for the music companies.

download	to transfer data from a central computer to another computer or to a terminal
file sharing	using files in common with other people
illegal	against the law
profit	the money made in a business
recording industry	business of making CDs
swap	to trade one thing for another; exchange
uploader	a person who transfers data, usually from a peripheral computer or device to a central computer or bulletin board

Comprehension

▸**EXERCISE 5 Read each statement. Then write *I agree because* or *I disagree because* and give a reason.**

1. It is fine for Brenda to download music free and then share it. *I agree because she doesn't make much money, and CDs are too expensive.*
2. Brenda thinks sharing music files is not illegal. ______________________
3. The music industry thinks that Brenda and other uploaders are thieves. ______________________
4. Brenda thinks CDs are not worth the high price. ______________________
5. The recording industry should sue the uploaders. ______________________

▶EXERCISE 6 Circle the letter of the main idea for each paragraph.

Paragraph 1:

a. The music industry makes too much money.

b. Downloading free music from the Internet is correct.

c. Brenda likes music but can't afford the recording industry's prices.

Paragraph 2:

a. The music industry is not doing anything wrong.

b. Because uploaders are only sharing music files, they don't think what they are doing is illegal.

c. Brenda and other uploaders are doing something legal.

Paragraph 3:

a. The RIAA sued file-sharing services and people for downloading music.

b. The RIAA sued the recording industry for providing free music files.

c. KaZaA and Napster sued the RIAA.

▶EXERCISE 7 Look at the answer first; then write the question.

1. *What does Brenda love to listen to?*

   Brenda loves to listen to music.

2. ______________________________?

   She can't afford the high CD prices that record companies charge.

3. ______________________________?

   Her solution is to download free music from the Internet.

4. ______________________________?

   People download free software from file-sharing services.

5. ______________________________?

   The music industry considers uploaders thieves.

6. ______________________________?

   File-sharing services allow people to download free software.

▶**EXERCISE 8** **Read the questions and answer them orally with your teacher. Then answer the questions orally with a classmate. At home, write the answers for homework. Answer in complete sentences.**

1. Why doesn't Brenda buy CDs? ______________________________

____

2. What is Brenda's solution? ______________________________

____

3. Where does she get the free file-sharing software programs? ______________________________

____

4. What do file-sharing services offer people? ______________________________

____

5. What do uploaders think about sharing music files with other people? ______________________________

____

6. Why do uploaders not want to pay $17–$20 per CD? ______________________________

____

7. What does Brenda do after she downloads the songs? ______________________________

____

8. What did the RIAA decide to do from 2001 to 2003? ______________________________

____

9. How much were the fines per song? ______________________________

____

10. Who said she did not know that it was illegal to download songs? ______________________________

____

11. What do you think about the prices of music CDs? ______________________________

____

12. What is your opinion about downloading music from the Internet? ______________________________

____

Vocabulary Practice

▶EXERCISE 9 Write T (true) or F (false) for each statement. Then discuss your answers with a classmate.

_____ 1. Trading free music files is the same as swapping free music files.

_____ 2. Downloading free music is the same as listening to free music.

_____ 3. A blank CD has many songs on it.

_____ 4. File-sharing software on the Internet allows you to download music.

_____ 5. When you sue someone, you take that person to court.

_____ 6. The profit a company makes is the money it loses.

_____ 7. A fine is not the same as a penalty or money you have to pay.

_____ 8. The music industry is made up of companies that record and sell music.

▶EXERCISE 10 Circle the letter of the correct answer.

1. Recording companies
   a. produce CDs and pay the artists.
   b. offer free music on the Internet.
   c. produce movies.
2. If you break the law, you are doing something that is
   a. legal.
   b. within the law.
   c. illegal.
3. Downloading music from the Internet is the same as
   a. copying music from the Internet.
   b. sharing music from the Internet.
   c. burning a CD.
4. What is the RIAA?
   a. The Recording Industry of American Artists.
   b. The Recording and Movie Industry Association of America.
   c. The Recording Industry Association of America.

5. *Sued* and *fined* mean
   a. taken to court and given money.
   b. taken to court and made to pay money.
   c. taken to court to represent a company.

6. Competition is
   a. companies that are in the same business.
   b. companies that are in different businesses.
   c. the different parts of one company.

Reading 2 Copyrighted Material and the Law

Before You Read

▸EXERCISE 11 Read each sentence; then circle agree or disagree.

1. *Legitimate* means "against the law." agree disagree
2. A penalty is the same as a fine. agree disagree
3. Shoplifting is stealing from a store. agree disagree

▸EXERCISE 12 Scan the reading; then write whose opinion it is.

1. They are just illegal freeloaders. ____________________
2. It is unfair for these people to steal my songs. ____________________
3. If you share songs, you should pay for them. ____________________
4. We should lower the prices of our CDs. ____________________
5. I am at the beginning of my career, and I want people to pay for my songs.
   ____
6. Most of the money from MerryRap's CD goes to us. ____________________
7. Stealing music over the Internet is like shoplifting. ____________________
8. We lowered the price of our CDs in 2003. ____________________

Words from the Reading*

penalty **shoplift**

*Your teacher can help you understand these words and others listed at the end of the chapter and on the Web site at http://esl.college.hmco.com/students.

Read to find out about a current controversy between the music industry and people who like to get free music.

Copyrighted Material and the Law

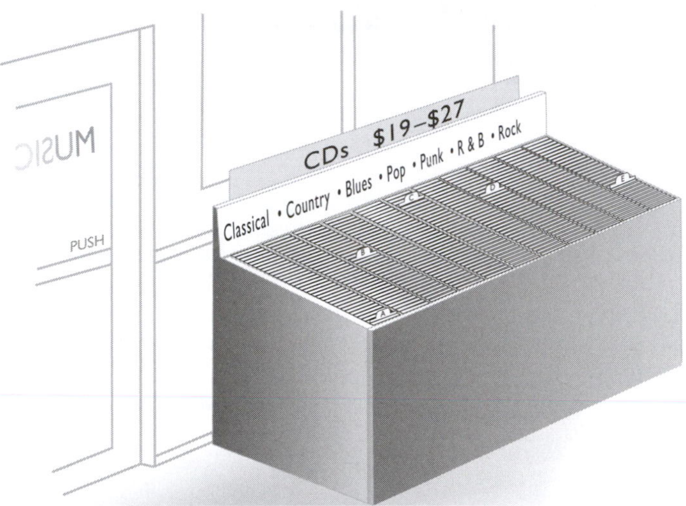

Karen and MerryRap are both in the entertainment business. They call people who share songs on the Internet illegal freeloaders, or people who take something that does not belong to them. Karen is an executive for the RIAA, and she is trying to stop the **unlawful** taking of copyrighted music over the Internet. A **copyright** gives a company or singer the exclusive, or only, right to copy or sell songs. MerryRap is a new but well-known rap singer who is just starting her career. Both the RIAA and entertainers in music are attempting to stop people from stealing their copyrighted work. At the same time, the recording industry is trying to take steps to **attract** customers.

MerryRap is completely against uploaders stealing her songs for free. She started singing in her church choir when she was only five years old. She always enjoyed singing and music, but her family could not always afford to buy her singing lessons. MerryRap continued practicing and performing her songs in school and in musical plays. After she worked very hard and performed anywhere she could, a record company agent saw her **perform** and heard some of her songs. The record company signed her to a small record contract. MerryRap recorded her first CD in 2003, and the sales have been very good. Many radio stations play her songs now. She thinks it is unfair and illegal for other people to steal songs that she worked so hard to record. She says she doesn't make much money yet because the record company keeps most of the money from her CD. MerryRap says that no one has the right to steal her songs.

Karen thinks the time for patience is over with the file-sharing services and the people who download and share music free over the Internet. The RIAA says that if you share a copyrighted song, you should pay for it, either with money or jail time. Karen thinks that the sixty million people all over the world who share music files would never walk into a music store and shoplift a CD. She thinks that stealing the music over the Internet is the same thing. The RIAA thinks both the file-sharing services and individuals should be fined and maybe jailed! In the summer of 2003, the U.S. House of Representatives introduced a bill that is very frightening for uploaders. The bill says that if you share even one downloaded song with your friends, you are a thief. The penalty is up to five years in jail!

The music industry is also trying to change its **image** of charging too much for CDs, at times **ripping off** artists, and is now offering music for sale on the Internet. In the fall of 2003, the world's largest record company decided to lower the price of many of its CDs to $12.98 instead of $17–$20. The reason was that the record industry lost money during a **sales slump,** which started in 2000 and continued into 2003. In 2003, the music industry started to offer individual songs for sale to customers over the Internet using services such as Apple iTunes Music Store, MusicNet, and the newest, Napster! Napster is now a legitimate company that sells songs online. Some of the legitimate companies charge one dollar or less per downloaded song. The music industry is hoping to attract customers legally, allow them to download individual songs at a cheaper price, and make money. It wants to offer music on the Internet that is of better quality than music from file-sharing services such as KaZaA. The music business is telling the public not to break the law and to respect the musical artists who write and record music.

attract	to cause someone or something to draw near
copyright	the legal right to be the only one to produce or sell an artistic work
image	the concept of something that is held by the public
perform	to present before an audience
rip off	to steal from
sales slump	a dip in the sale of an item
unlawful	against the law

Comprehension

▸EXERCISE 13 Write T (true) or F (false) for each statement.

_____ 1. MerryRap and Karen are in the entertainment business.

_____ 2. Karen is an executive with RIAA, and MerryRap sings with her.

_____ 3. A copyright protects a singer or company.

_____ 4. A freeloader gives away things to people for free.

_____ 5. The music industry and entertainers are trying to stop uploaders.

_____ 6. MerryRap recorded her first CDs many years ago and is wealthy.

_____ 7. MerryRap thinks it is fine for people to download her songs for free.

_____ 8. Karen wants uploaders to pay for the music they take.

_____ 9. Karen says downloading music is the same as shoplifting a CD.

_____ 10. Napster is now offering free songs on the Internet again.

▸EXERCISE 14 Circle the letter of the main idea for each paragraph.

Paragraph 1:

a. Karen and MerryRap are both popular singers but are new singers.

b. Karen and MerryRap are in the music business and are against uploaders.

c. Karen and MerryRap have different opinions about illegal freeloaders.

Paragraph 2:

a. MerryRap is a very wealthy and experienced singer.

b. MerryRap is at the beginning of her career and doesn't want freeloaders to steal her songs for free.

c. MerryRap starting singing in her church and at school.

Paragraph 3:

a. Karen is impatient with file-sharing services and uploaders.

b. Karen is impatient with music companies that charge too much for CDs.

c. Karen is patient about the CD sales slump.

Paragraph 4:

a. The music industry is having a sales slump.

b. The music industry is changing about its image, about ripping off artists, and about offering music on the Internet.

c. The music industry is suing people for downloading music.

▸EXERCISE 15 Read the questions, and answer them orally with your teacher. Then answer the questions orally with a classmate. At home, write the answers for homework. Answer in complete sentences.

Paragraph 1:

1. What do MerryRap and Karen agree about? ______________________________

____

2. What is a freeloader? ______________________________

____

3. What is a copyright on a song? ______________________________

____

Paragraph 2:

4. How and where did MerryRap start singing? ______________________________

____

5. How are sales of her first CD? ______________________________

____

6. What is her opinion about people who steal her copyrighted songs? ______________

____

7. Who plays her songs now? ______________________________

____

Paragraph 3:

8. What does Karen, the RIAA executive, want for downloaders and the file-sharing services? ______________________________

____

9. What does the RIAA want to happen? ______________________________

____

10. What does the House of Representatives bill say? ______________________________

____

11. Who does the RIAA want to put in jail? ______________________________

____

Paragraph 4:

12. What did the music industry start to offer on the Internet in 2003? ______________

____

13. Why is it legal for Napster to now offer songs on the Internet? ______________

____

14. Who does the record industry want the public to respect? ______________

____

15. Is Napster still an illegal company? Explain. ______________________________

____

Vocabulary Practice

▶EXERCISE 16 Write a synonym for each underlined word. Choose words from "Copyrighted Material and the Law."

Paragraph 1:

1. People who swap songs for free are unlawful freeloaders. ____________________
2. A singer has the exclusive right to copy or sell her songs. ____________________
3. People who sing or play music are worried now. ____________________

Paragraph 2:

4. MerryRap's parents could not pay for expensive lessons. ____________________
5. She sang her songs at school and in musical plays. ____________________
6. MerryRap believes that is it very unjust to steal her songs. ____________________

Paragraph 3:

7. The RIAA say that if you swap a song, you are a thief. ____________________
8. The RIAA thinks that downloaders should serve prison time. ____________________
9. Karen thinks that people would never steal from a store. ____________________

Paragraph 4:

10. The RIAA is trying to change what the public thinks of it. ____________________
11. Sometimes the music industry pays little money to artists. ____________________
12. The music industry is having low sales of its CDs. ____________________

▶EXERCISE 17 Read the explanation. Write the underlined word with the prefix indicated.

Prefixes are letters at the beginning of a word that change the meaning of the word.

Prefix	New Word
dis- **(not, no)** *He is not an agreeable person.*	**disagreeable**
il- **(not, no)** *Your writing is not legible.*	**illegible**

Use the prefix *il-:*

1. The RIAA thinks downloading music is not legal. ____________________
2. Napster's business was not legitimate before. ____________________
3. What the man is saying is not logical. ____________________
4. In some countries, nonliteracy is a problem. ____________________

Use the prefix *dis-:*

5. The music industry and the downloaders do not agree. ____________________
6. The RIAA does not approve of free file-sharing services. ____________________
7. They was no agreement in court. ____________________
8. The court did not allow Napster to continue in 2001. ____________________

Expansion Activities

▸ Activity 1 Check Out Those New Legal Music Sites! *In groups of four, each person chooses a legal music site on the Internet: iTunes Music Store, Napster, RealOne Rhapsody, musicmatch, or MusicNet. Research the following information about your music site:*

a. Is there a monthly subscription?

____

b. Can you buy and download albums? What is the price?

____

c. What is the price per download of individual songs?

____

d. What are the special features of your site?

____

On separate paper, write a short paragraph about what you found out, and share the information with your group.

► **Activity 2 Conduct a Survey** *Would your classmates download free music from file-sharing services? Ask ten of your classmates which they would use, a pay-for legal downloading service or a free file-sharing service such as KaZaA, and why. Summarize your findings in a short paragraph.*

Vocabulary List

Adjectives

copyrighted
entertainment
exclusive
free
frightening
illegal
shared
strict
unlawful

Adverbs

really
recently
ridiculously

Nouns

artist
choir
company/companies
competition
copyright
customer
entertainer
expense
fine
freeloader
image
industry
law
lawsuit
patience
penalty
profit
quality/qualities
recording industry
sales slump
solution
thief

Technical Terms

burn a CD
downloader
file-sharing
online
software
uploader

Verbs—Present Tense

afford
attract
belong
break the law
charge
consider
download
jail
love
lower
perform
respect
rip off
share
shoplift
shut down
sue
trade

Verbs—Past Tense

fined
introduced
sued
swapped
traded

If you want to review vocabulary and complete additional activities related to this chapter, go to the *Read to Succeed 2* Web site at http://esl.college.hmco.com/students.

CHAPTER 11

Diet, Exercise, and Fitness

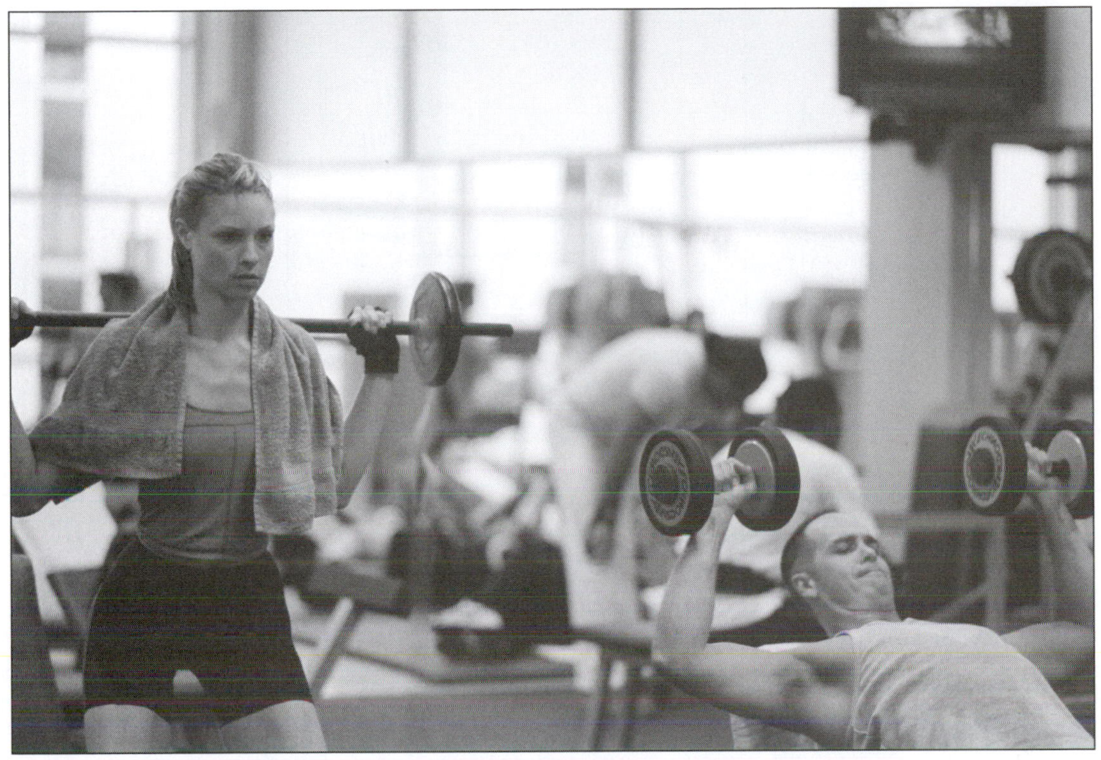

Reading 1 Here's to Your Health!

Before You Read

▶**EXERCISE 1 Discuss these questions with a partner or a small group.**

1. What is a healthful meal for you?
2. How often do you exercise?
3. What types of exercise do you like to do?
4. Where do people exercise more, in your native country or in the United States?
5. Do you eat healthful foods every day?

▶**EXERCISE 2 Look at the following pictures; then write the letter of the picture next to the sentence that describes it.**

A.

B.

C.

D.

A good idea—a balanced diet from these food groups:

1. We should eat three to five portions of vegetables and two to four servings of fruit per day. ______
2. Dairy products are an essential part of every diet. ______
3. Bread, cereals, and grains are important to our health. ______
4. Meat, fish, and chicken provide us with protein and other necessary nutrients. ______

Not a good idea for your health:

A.

B.

C.

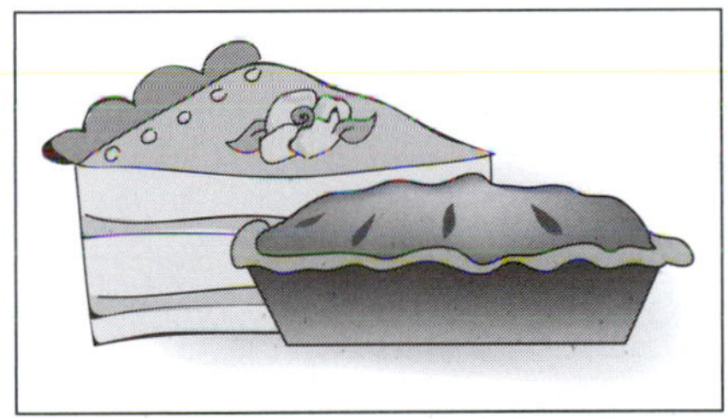

D.

E.

F.

5. A lot of fatty meats are not good for the body. ______
6. Eating fast food is the reason many people don't get the nutrients they need. ______
7. Sugar and sweets should be eaten only sparingly. ______
8. Too much alcohol is dangerous for our health. ______
9. Doctors tell us to avoid a lot of coffee and caffeinated drinks. ______
10. Nicotine is bad for our health. ______

▶EXERCISE 3 Write a short answer to each question.

1. When we see the word "Caution" on a sign, we need to be ________________.
2. Inside our body we have ________________ to give our body support and ________________ to move our body with.
3. Each day we need some ________________ or servings of fruits and vegetables.

Words from the Reading*

bone	**play catch**
heart	**surgeon general**
hide-and-seek	**sweet**
muscle	**portions**

*Your teacher can help you understand these words and others listed at the end of the chapter and on the Web site at http://esl.college.hmco.com/students.

▶EXERCISE 4 Scan the reading and answer the questions.

1. How much time should people try to exercise each week? ________________

____

2. What is one recommendation of the U.S. Surgeon General? ________________

____

3. What is one benefit of exercise? ________________

____

Read to learn about the importance of exercising and eating right for your health.

Here's to Your Health!

Do you want to look younger? Do you want to feel strong, avoid illness, and **reduce** stress? Of course, most of us want all of these things, but often we think that to **achieve** these goals, we need to drink a magical potion! No, you don't need to drink any magical potion; you just need to drink water, exercise often, eat right, get **enough** sleep, **avoid** smoking, be **cautious** about alcohol consumption, and visit a doctor **regularly.** Who said that it was going to be simple? So how do you begin? By exercising regularly and eating right.

Regular exercise will greatly improve your health. First, consult with your doctor before beginning any exercise program. Choose an exercise that's interesting for you. Many people start with walking—it's cheap and easy! With any exercise, start slowly and **build up** to exercising twenty to sixty minutes three to five times a week. If you don't have that much time all at once, then break up your exercise into ten-minute routines spread out over the day. **Incorporate** exercise into your daily routine: take the stairs instead of an elevator, or park at a farther distance from your job or school and walk farther. If you have children, exercising can be a family activity. Get yourself and your children doing some physical activity every day or at least every day that you can spend time together. Play catch, tag, or hide-and-seek, or take a walk together in place of watching television or playing video games. Make it a point to do a fun physical activity every day, even if only for ten minutes.

Eating right is extremely important for your health. A good diet, along with regular exercise, can mean the difference between health and sickness. The U.S. Surgeon General has recommended that people eat three to five **portions** of vegetables, two to four **servings** of fruit, two to three servings of protein, two to three servings of dairy products, and six to eleven servings of breads and cereals every day. These recommendations also advise using fats, oils, and sweets **sparingly.** Most people have the hardest time making sure that they eat the correct number and variety of vegetable portions. Many doctors tell people that they should try to eat vegetables at every meal and in different colors to make sure that they get the correct **nutrients.** The quality of the food that we eat matters too; the whole grains found in whole-wheat bread, for example, are much more healthful than white bread. Fast foods are one reason that people today are overweight; you need to take the time to prepare meals that give you the nutrients you need. To limit **calorie** intake, stay away from second servings, except for vegetables. A reduced-calorie diet can be very effective in helping people to live healthier and lose weight, but it's important to remember that a **drastic** reduction of calories should only be done under the supervision of a doctor. The best way to lose weight is **gradually,** through a combination of moderate exercise and a healthy diet.

It's obvious that eating right and exercising regularly are very **beneficial.** Eating good foods makes you feel great and helps prevent many types of illnesses. Exercise makes your body release chemicals called endorphins, which reduce stress and cause you to feel better emotionally. Exercise tones muscles, helps the body to support the spine, and produces healthier bones, lungs, and heart. Now doesn't that sound like a magical potion?

achieve	to succeed in completing, producing, or gaining something	**gradually**	slowly, little by little
		incorporate	to include
avoid	to keep away from something	**nutrient**	something in food that nourishes
beneficial	helpful		
build up	to increase	**portion**	an amount of food
calorie	a unit for measuring the amount of heat energy supplied by food	**reduce**	to make less
		regularly	usually or normally
cautious	careful	**serving**	a single portion of food or drink
drastic	severe or extreme in nature		
enough	able to meet a need	**sparingly**	in small amounts

Comprehension

▸EXERCISE 5 Write T (true) or F (false) for each statement. Then discuss your answers with a classmate.

_____ 1. To be healthy, you just need a magical potion.

_____ 2. People need to get enough sleep every night.

_____ 3. When you begin to exercise, it's good to exercise long and hard immediately.

_____ 4. You should exercise at least twenty to sixty minutes three to five times a week.

_____ 5. There are many ways to include exercise in your daily routine.

_____ 6. The Surgeon General recommends the same number of portions of all kinds of food.

_____ 7. Eating vegetables in a variety of colors is not a good idea.

_____ 8. The best way to lose weight is to eat very little food.

_____ 9. Eating right can prevent many kinds of health problems.

_____ 10. Endorphins are chemicals in our body that affect our emotions.

_____ 11. Exercise is important; a good diet is less important.

_____ 12. You cannot exercise at work.

_____ 13. Incorporate is the same as add.

_____ 14. Eating less and exercising more can make you gain weight.

▸EXERCISE 6 Complete the sentence to tell the main idea of each paragraph.

Paragraph 1: If you want to be healthier, two important ______________________.

Paragraph 2: There are many ways to ______________________.

Paragraph 3: Eating right is important because ______________________.

Paragraph 4: By eating right and exercising, ______________________.

►EXERCISE 7 Complete the charts with three details about each idea from "Here's to Your Health!"

Diet

Surgeon General Recommendations	*3–5 portions of vegetables* *2–4 servings of fruit* *Use fats, oils, and sweets sparingly*
Quality of food	
Calories	
To lose weight	

Exercise

Starting to exercise	
Daily routine	
Exercising with family	
Exercising at work	

►EXERCISE 8 Read the questions, and answer them orally with your teacher. Then answer them orally with a classmate. At home, write the answers for homework. Answer in complete sentences.

About the Reading

1. What is one very cheap, easy, and popular exercise? ______________________

____

2. What are some ways to incorporate exercise into your daily routine? ______________________

____

3. What do many doctors recommend about vegetables? ______________________

____

4. How much should we eat of foods that have fats, oils, or sweets? ______________________

____

5. What is the best way to lose weight? ______________________

____

6. How does exercise make us feel better emotionally? ______________________

____

7. What effect does exercise have on our muscles and bones? ______________________

____

8. What is wrong with fast food? ______________________

____

About You

9. What are your favorite vegetables? ______________________

____

10. Have you felt the benefits of exercise when you have exercised? ______________________

____

11. What activities do you do with your family? ______________________

____

12. Did your mother cook vegetables for you? Do you cook them for your children now?

____

Vocabulary

▸EXERCISE 9 Complete each sentence with a word from the box.

A.

achieve	cautious	incorporate	enough	gradually	regular

1. ________________ she has learned to speak English; she has worked hard for a long time.
2. He never has ________________ time to exercise every day.
3. I'm going to work hard to ________________ my goals.
4. It's important to find time to ________________ exercise into the time you spend with your family.
5. You should be ________________ about exercising at first. Don't do too much at the beginning.
6. ________________ exercise is good for our health.

B.

sparingly	sweets	spine	heart	builds up	portions

7. Children usually love to eat ________________.
8. Parents should buy candy for their children very ________________.
9. Stress ________________ over time; we need to release it before it becomes a problem.
10. The ________________ is a muscle too.
11. The ________________ is an important bone in our body.
12. We should eat several ________________ of vegetables each day.

Grammar Hints: Past Participle in the Present Perfect for Regular Verbs

For the past participle for regular verbs, add *-ed* or *-d*:

talked decided

In the present perfect tense, *have/has* + the past participle shows

- what has happened already at an indefinite time or what has happened repeatedly (many times):

I have talked to the doctor. She has visited many doctors.
They have not asked questions. He has not decided yet.

- what started in the past and still continues:

I have lived here for years. She has not worked there before.

I have not prepared dinner.

▸EXERCISE 10 Complete each sentence with a present perfect verb from the box.

has visited	have talked	have not lived	has worked
has not asked	have wanted	has discussed	have not delivered

1. Paul and Sandra ______________________ a baby for nine years.
2. Raoul ______________________ investments with his financial advisor.
3. Gina and Rob ______________________ to their families about moving overseas.
4. We ______________________ in our house for a long time.
5. Maria ______________________ at the same company for five years.
6. My boss ______________________ me about making that decision.
7. Shelly ______________________ Australia and New Zealand.
8. They ______________________ the pizza yet.

Reading 2 What's on the Exercise Menu Today?

Before You Read

▸EXERCISE 11 Write a short answer to complete each sentence.

1. The body's muscles gently ________________ in yoga.
2. Aerobics tones ________________ and burns ________________.
3. Rock climbing can be done indoors or ________________.
4. Breathing and stretching are important when we ________________.

▸EXERCISE 12 Scan the reading and answer these questions.

1. What are two exercises that emphasize relaxation? ________________
2. In what exercise do people tone muscles and burn calories to the beat of music? ________________
3. What is an indoor form of cycling? ________________
4. What are some things to learn in rock climbing? ________________
5. Where does Zoe like to go after work? ________________
6. Are there many or few people at the gym? ________________
7. What classes does she take at the gym? ________________
8. What is spinning at the gym? ________________

Words from the Reading*

breathing **stretch**
gear **weight**
outdoors

*Your teacher can help you understand these words and others listed at the end of the chapter and on the Web site at http://esl.college.hmco.com/students.

Read to find out about different kinds of exercise.

What's on the Exercise Menu Today?

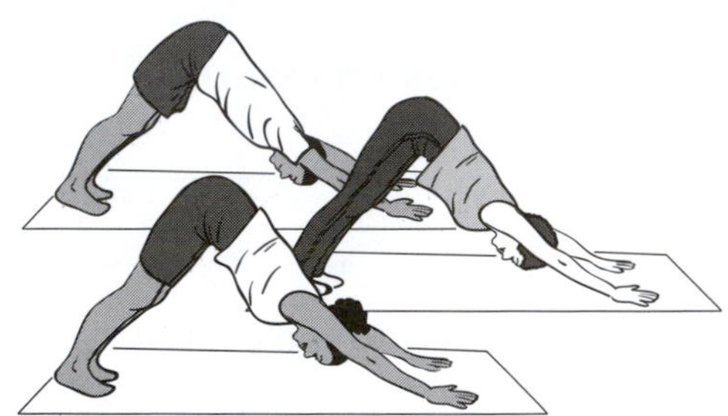

Zoe gets out of work at 5:00 PM every day and **heads for** the local gym. As she walks through the door, she sees that she has **plenty of company.** The gym is filled with people like Zoe who want to **get or keep in shape.** But don't think that Zoe and the many people she meets there are at the gym only to lift weights. In addition to weight training, gyms today offer a variety of exercise possibilities.

In a quiet room in one corner of the gym, Zoe can take yoga or pilates classes. Yoga and pilates are two activities that help increase **flexibility** and **strength,** reduce stress, and relax the body and mind. Yoga has been practiced for thousands of years. Traditional yoga emphasizes a slow, **gentle** stretch. Pilates places importance on strengthening stomach and back muscles, which many people have found helps to improve **posture.** Both yoga and pilates use special breathing techniques.

Jazz, salsa, and hip-hop are just a few of the types of music that gym members can enjoy while doing aerobics. This type of exercise **tones** muscles and burns calories to the beat of music. An aerobics class typically begins with ten to fifteen minutes of warm-up exercises done at a low to moderate speed and moves to a faster-paced exercise that uses the body's large muscle groups in continuous movement. This gives the heart, lungs, and cardiovascular system the workout that they need. An aerobics class will always end with a cool-down exercise and stretching and relaxation activities. Some aerobics classes are even held in the water! Aerobics is fun and great for your health. Zoe used to notice that only women took aerobics classes, but now more and more men have gotten interested in aerobics classes as well.

Have you ever been interested in cycling? Have you worried that you're not in shape yet for a long bike ride? Or has bad weather been keeping you inside? Try a spinning class! Zoe attends one at her gym. She and several other students sit on a special bike and follow instructions from a spinning teacher. The students change the gears on the bike to **simulate** riding uphill or downhill. It's quite a workout!

Not everyone lives close to a mountain where they can go rock climbing, but since indoor climbing walls have become more common in gyms, people are able to take part in rock climbing year-round. This sport builds strong arms and shoulders and increases flexibility. There's a lot to learn with rock climbing. How to use the equipment properly, safety, and communication are just a few important aspects of rock climbing. Group rock-climbing trips are often used for building trust and teamwork. Of course, rock climbers can train for rock climbing outdoors by starting indoors at a gym.

At the gym, Zoe may try out an aerobics class and another day enroll in a spinning class. Zoe **keeps on top of** all the new offerings at her gym because she doesn't want to miss out on anything new. She feels great after a workout; it's good for her health, she has made new friends, and there is always something new to try.

flexibility	the capability to be bent or changed
gentle	mild and soft
get (keep) in shape	to become (stay) in good physical health and condition
head for	to go to
keep on top of	to stay aware of
plenty of company	a lot of people doing the same thing
posture	the way in which one holds one's body
simulate	to imitate
strength	the quality of being strong
tone	to make stronger and firmer

Comprehension

▸EXERCISE 13 Write T (true) or F (false) for each statement. Then discuss your answers with your classmates.

______ 1. There are many different ways to exercise at a gym.

______ 2. Pilates and aerobics use special breathing techniques.

______ 3. An aerobics class does not include a warm-up and cool-down part.

______ 4. Aerobics are always held in the water.

______ 5. Aerobics gives the heart and lungs a healthy workout.

______ 6. Spinning is always held outside.

______ 7. Rock climbing builds trust and teamwork among people.

______ 8. One of the things that rock climbing improves is arm and shoulder strength.

______ 9. Indoor climbing walls have become more popular.

______ 10. Increased flexibility is a benefit of yoga, pilates, aerobics, and rock climbing.

▸EXERCISE 14 Imagine that you are explaining each of the types of exercises below to a friend. Write the three most important ideas about each exercise that you would tell your friend.

1. Yoga
   a. *Yoga increases flexibility and strength.*
   b. ______
   c. ______
2. Aerobics
   a. ______
   b. ______
   c. ______
3. Spinning
   a. ______
   b. ______
   c. ______
4. Rock climbing
   a. ______
   b. ______
   c. ______

▸EXERCISE 15 Read the questions and answer them orally with your teacher. Then answer them orally with a classmate. At home, write the answers for homework. Answer in complete sentences.

About the Reading

1. What are the benefits of yoga and pilates? ______
2. What are the three parts of an aerobics class? ______

3. What do students do in a spinning class? ______

4. What do people learn from rock climbing? ______

5. Where can people do rock climbing? ______

6. What are some advantages of working out in a gym? ______

7. What does Zoe try not to miss out on? ______

About You

8. Have you ever tried going to a gym? What was your experience there? ______

9. Which of the types of exercises in the reading interest you? Why? ______

10. What types of activities are best for making friends? Sports or exercise? School? Social events? Explain. ______

Vocabulary Practice

▶EXERCISE 16 On separate paper, write an original sentence using each vocabulary word or phrase. Share your sentences with a classmate.

1. flexibility
2. burn calories
3. tone muscles
4. simulate
5. posture
6. strength
7. keep on top of
8. work out
9. gentle
10. head (verb)

▸EXERCISE 17

A. Add the prefix *in-* before the words in parentheses.

in appropriate (not appropriate)

1. Jack is very ____________________ (flexible) about his diet. He will not change it.
2. Jack is ____________________ (active) and just sits and watches television.
3. Jack is ____________________ (capable) of running three miles. He is too overweight.

B. Add the prefix *un-* before the words in parentheses.

un safe (not safe)

4. Maria is in good condition, but Jack is ____________________ (fit) and overweight.
5. An ____________________ (healthy) diet is very dangerous.
6. Jack eats too many fatty foods, so his diet is ____________________ (balanced).
7. Artificial colors, flavors, and preservatives are ____________________ (natural).

Reading Charts and Graphs

▸EXERCISE 18

A. Read the information in this chart and answer the questions.

Statistics on Overweight People in the United States*

61% of adults (20 years old or older)	Overweight or obese
14% of adolescents (12–19 years old)	Overweight
13% of children (6–11 years old)	Overweight

*United States National Center for Health Statistics, 1999.

1. What percentage of American adults are overweight or obese? ____________________
2. What percentage of adolescents are overweight? ____________________
3. Are overweight children a problem in the United States? ____________________

B. Read the information in this chart and answer the questions.

Causes of Death and Risk Behaviors in the United States*

Causes of Death Each Year in the United States	Number of Deaths Each Year
Cardiovascular disease (heart)—41%	1,000,000 people
Cancer—23.6%	550,000 people

Risk Behaviors in the United States	Number of Deaths Each Year
Smoking and tobacco	430,000 people
Poor diet	300,000 people
Injuries, sexual violence, and physical inactivity	No statistics available

*Centers for Disease Control and Prevention, 1999 statistics.

4. How many people die from cardiovascular disease each year? ____________________
5. What is the number-two cause of death? ____________________
6. What percentage of people in the United States die from cancer each year?

   ____
7. What kills about 400,000 people each year? ____________________
8. How many people die from poor diet each year? ____________________
9. Are there statistics for physical inactivity? ____________________
10. How many people die from smoking each year? ____________________
11. Where do these statistics come from? ____________________
12. What should you do (or not do) to improve your health? ____________________

    ____

C. Read the information in this chart and answer the questions.

Statistics on Inactivity in the United States*

Do not exercise regularly	60%
Do not exercise at all (all ages)	25%
Do not exercise at all (12–21 years old)	50%
Inactivity increases with age	Particularly for low-income and low-education populations
New technology increases inactivity	Video, DVD, computers, and television

*Centers for Disease Control and Prevention, 1999 statistics.

11. What percentage of Americans do not exercise regularly? ________________
12. How many people of all ages do not exercise at all? ________________
13. What percentage of people ages twelve to twenty-one do not exercise at all? ________________
14. Does new technology increase or decrease inactivity? ________________
15. How is inactivity related to age? ________________

Expansion Activities

►**Activity 1 Create a Health Commercial** *With a partner or small group, create a 30- or 60-second television commercial for a healthy food or drink, or for an exercise or a healthy activity. Describe why the product or activity is good by using the vocabulary in this lesson. Present the commercial to your class. Demonstrate the product or activity as you speak. Then have the students vote "yes" or "no" if they would like to try this product or activity.*

►**Activity 2 How Healthy Are Your Classmates?** *Using the information that you know about a healthy diet and exercise, think of three questions to ask your classmates about their diet and health. For example, "How often do you do cardiovascular exercises?" Write a paragraph about what you learned about your classmates' habits from the survey.*

Vocabulary List

Adjectives
beneficial
cautious
drastic
effective
gentle
healthful
magical
moderate
overweight
quiet

Adverbs
emotionally
enough
extremely
gradually
great
regularly
sparingly

Nouns
activity/activities
arm
breathing
calorie
catch
cycling
exercise
fat
flexibility
gear
heart
hide-and-seek
illness
instruction
muscle
nutrient
oil
outdoors
plenty of company
portion
posture
potion
routine
serving
shoulder
strength
stretch
supervision
surgeon general
sweet
tag
teamwork
variety
weight

Verbs
achieve
advise
ask
avoid
break up
build up
burn
describe
eat
exercise
get (keep) in shape
head for
incorporate
keep on top of
meet
play
play catch
prepare
reduce
simulate
talk
tone
visit
work

If you want to review vocabulary and complete additional activities related to this chapter, go to the *Read to Succeed 2* Web site at http://esl.college.hmco.com/students.

CHAPTER 12

Emergency Medical Measures

Reading 1 Medical Emergency Angels

Before You Read

▶EXERCISE 1 Discuss these questions with a partner or a small group.

1. In your native country, what emergency workers respond to accidents on the street?
2. What examples can you give of problems with drinking and driving?
3. When should you call 911?
4. In your family, who makes the decisions in a serious medical emergency?

▸EXERCISE 2 Emergency medical technician paramedics and hospital staff have difficult jobs. Look at the following pictures; then write the letter of the picture next to the sentence that describes it.

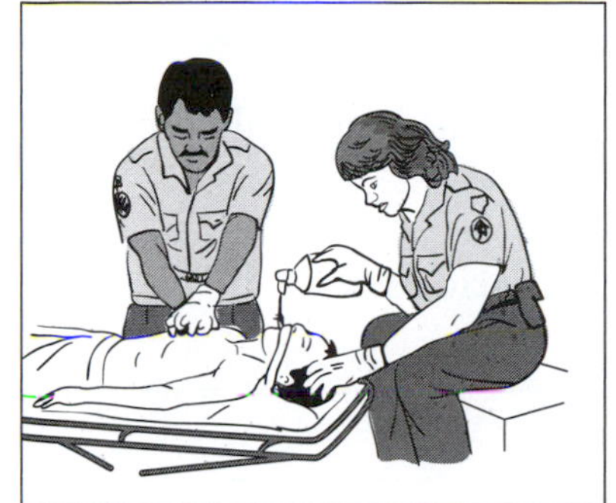

A.

B.

C.

D.

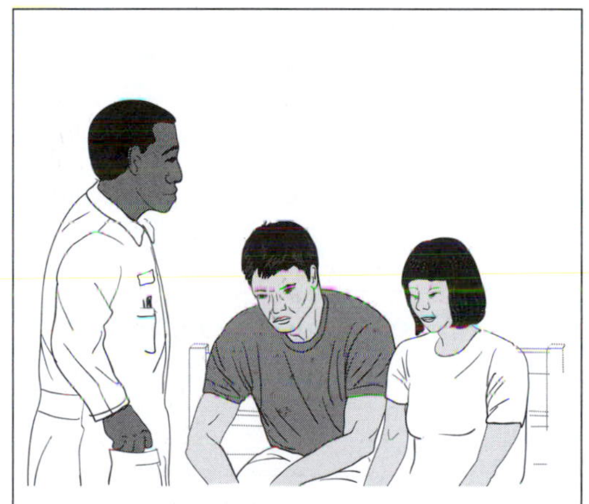

E.

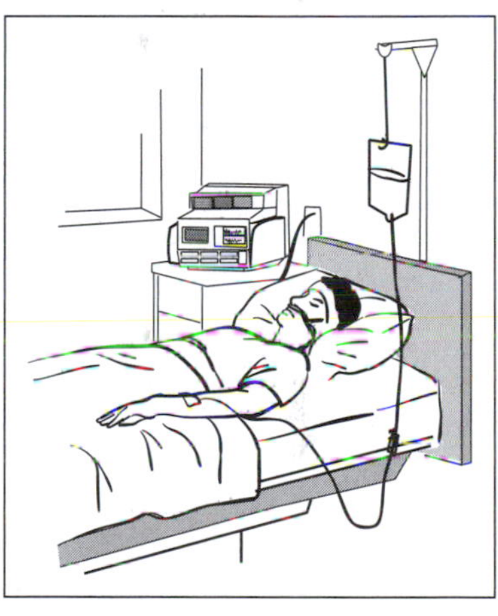

F.

1. Sometimes machines keep a person alive. ______
2. Doctors look at the results of tests and X-rays to decide what to do. ______
3. The doctor tells the boy's parents, "The boy is in a coma, and he can't. . . ." ______
4. Paramedics transport injured people to hospitals. ______
5. The doctors discuss the boy's serious injuries. ______
6. An EMT sometimes uses CPR. ______

▸EXERCISE 3 Draw a line to match the term with the definition.

1. brain-dead
2. life-support machines
3. EMT paramedics
4. antonym for *alive*

a. machines that keep you alive
b. condition in which the brain does not function
c. dead
d. people who give emergency medical help

▸EXERCISE 4 Scan the reading and answer the questions.

1. What kind of job does Clara have? ______________________________

____

2. What kind of accident did the two EMTs respond to? ______________________________

____

3. What was the male victim's condition at the hospital? ______________________________

____

4. What education does a person need to become a paramedic? ______________________________

____

5. Does an EMT require more or less training and classes than other paramedics? ______

____

6. What does CPR do for a person? ______________________________

____

7. What was the victim's name and age? ______________________________

____

8. What was helping David breathe?______________________________

____

Words from the Reading*

brain-dead **life-support machine**
EMT paramedic

*Your teacher can help you understand these words and others listed at the end of the chapter and on the Web site at http://esl.college.hmco.com/students.

Read to learn about special people who help in medical emergencies.

Medical Emergency Angels

An emergency medical technician paramedic has one of the most important and interesting jobs in the medical field. Many people consider them medical emergency angels. Most EMT paramedics work for private ambulance services, hospitals, city governments, or fire departments. They usually work in teams. EMT paramedics receive the highest of four levels of training for emergency medical personnel.* They must be very calm in emergencies, clear thinking, and physically strong. They have provided the public with life-or-death assistance, many times away from a hospital, and they have seen many accidents, heart attacks, gunshot victims, and childbirths. This job can be very stressful, but most of the time it is enjoyable and **rewarding.**

There are several requirements before a person can work as an EMT paramedic. A degree from a community college is necessary to work as a paramedic, and to become an EMT paramedic, advanced training classes and tests are required to demonstrate competence. These medical emergency angels have saved many people through **cardiopulmonary resuscitation (CPR),** which means that they start a person's heart beating again and the lungs breathing normally. They have assisted people with a variety of other medical emergency problems: they have stopped a person's bleeding, they have given people oxygen, and they have injected people with the appropriate drugs.* This job can be stressful when EMT paramedics deal with tragic traffic accidents and with patients who have mental instabilities, contagious diseases, and drug overdoses.*

Two weeks ago, Clara, an EMT paramedic, responded to a serious accident in which a drunk driver had hit a young man on a motorcycle. When Clara and her partner arrived, the police were assisting the victim, and they were also keeping people away from the accident. Clara quickly **assessed** the male victim's condition. He was about twenty years old, and he was **unconscious.** He was not breathing, he was bleeding in the head area, and his heart was beating weakly. While Clara was giving the young man CPR, her partner stopped the bleeding. Then her partner checked the victim's pulse while she was giving him mouth-to-mouth resuscitation. Since his heartbeat was so weak, she decided to use the manual defibrillator, which started the heart beating strongly once more. The young man's breathing was

*U.S. Department of Labor, Bureau of Labor Statistics, 2003.

not responding. They put him on a backboard, then a stretcher, quickly loaded him into the ambulance, and rushed him to the hospital emergency room. Clara continued pulmonary resuscitation in the ambulance on the way to the hospital. The police found empty beer bottles in the drunk driver's car, so they took him to jail.

The young man's condition remained very critical in the emergency room. While Clara was speaking to the doctor, the hospital staff looked at his identification and telephoned his parents. His name was David, and he was twenty-one years old, single, and a college student. Life-support machines were helping David to breathe, and another machine showed no brain activity. The doctors said David had horrible head and lung injuries and was in very serious condition. They rushed David to surgery to save him. After the unsuccessful operation, the doctor said there was no **hope** for David. Some of his organs were strong and healthy, but he was brain-dead. After a week, he was still in a coma and on life-support machines. The doctors were feeding David through tubes, and without the machines, David would die. His family very sadly decided to turn off the machines. They wanted David to die naturally because he was not going to recover. The doctor spoke to them about **organ donation.** David was legally an adult, but he did not have a **will** or an organ donor card with his driver's license. A **decision** about organ donation had to be made.

assess	to analyze and determine significance or value
CPR (cardiopulmonary resuscitation)	a way to get the heart and lungs working again
decision	a conclusion or judgment
hope	confidence, faith, belief
organ donation	the gift of an organ of a deceased person to a live person for transplant
rewarding	offering satisfaction
unconscious	unable to move, feel, or respond
will	a legal document stating how a person wishes to give out his or her money and possessions after death

Comprehension

▶EXERCISE 5 Write the sentence from each paragraph that summarizes the paragraph the best. A summary gives all the main points of the paragraph in one sentence.

Paragraph 1:

____

Paragraph 2:

____

Paragraph 3:

Paragraph 4:

▶**EXERCISE 6** **Read the questions and answer them orally with your teacher. Then answer the questions orally with a classmate. At home, write the answers for homework. Answer in complete sentences.**

1. What does an EMT paramedic do? ______
2. What requirements must an EMT paramedic have? ______
3. What does CPR stand for? ______
4. What do *cardio* and *pulmonary* mean? ______
5. What did Clara use at the accident scene to strengthen David's heartbeat? ______
6. Why was David on life-support machines? ______
7. Why did his parents decide to turn off the life-support machines? ______
8. Why do you think David did not have an organ donor card? ______
9. What kind of medical emergencies do paramedics and EMTs see? ______
10. What type of person becomes a paramedic or EMT? ______

▶EXERCISE 7 Number the sentences in the correct sequence. Number 1 is what happened first, and number 11 is what happened last.

_____ a. David's condition remained the same at the emergency room.

_____ b. Clara quickly assessed the male victim's condition.

__1__ c. Clara graduated as a paramedic from a community college.

_____ d. There was no hope for David after the operation.

_____ e. She and her partner provided CPR to the young victim.

_____ f. The man in the car had been drinking alcohol that day.

_____ g. Clara took many advanced classes and tests to become an EMT.

_____ h. The EMT paramedics loaded David into the ambulance.

__11__ i. The doctor spoke to David's parents about organ donation.

_____ j. The drunk man's car hit David on his motorcycle.

_____ k. Clara and her partner responded to the accident.

Vocabulary Practice

▶EXERCISE 8 Complete the paragraph with words from the box.

have provided	life-or-death	degree	CPR
pulmonary	physically	heart attacks	competence
drug overdose	contagious disease	level	stressful

An EMT Paramedic's Job

An EMT paramedic's job is at the highest ______________ of emergency medical personnel away from a hospital. Through the years, EMT paramedics ______________ assistance to people in medical emergencies. ______________ has been necessary at many medical emergency scenes. EMT paramedics see many ______________ and at times have to use the manual defibrillator to start a person's heart again. They also use ________________ to start people's lungs breathing. An EMT paramedic has to kneel, bend, and lift all day, so ________________, they have to be in very good condition. Clara's quick ________________ assistance has saved many people. She receives satisfaction from the service she provides to people in emergencies, and she is glad she obtained her ________________ from the community college. She is one of the best in her profession, and she shows her ________________ every day. The only ________________ part of her job is when she has to assist a drug addict with a ________________ or a person with a ________________ like AIDS or Hepatitis B.

▸EXERCISE 9 Write a synonym for each underlined word. Choose from words found in "Medical Emergency Angels."

Paragraph 1:

1. Clara has given assistance to people. ________________

Paragraph 2:

2. A degree from a community college is required. ________________
3. Clara shows her ability every day. ________________
4. EMT paramedics sometime inject people with the right drugs ________________

Paragraph 3:

5. The EMTs went to an accident. ________________
6. Clara and her partner got there after the police. ________________
7. The ambulance hurried the victim to the hospital. ________________

Paragraph 4:

8. David's condition stayed the same. ________________
9. His heart and kidneys were strong. ________________
10. They decided to unplug the machines. ________________

Grammar Hints: The Past Progressive

The past progressive tense

was or *were* + verb ending in *ing*

describes what was happening in the past at a certain time, or while another action happened.

Clara was studying in college when she decided to be a paramedic.
While the EMTs were cleaning their equipment, the phone rang.
David was not breathing.

►EXERCISE 10 Complete each sentence with the past progressive form of the verb in parentheses.

1. David ____________________ (bleed) from his head when Clara arrived.
2. Soon after David arrived at the hospital, the doctors ____________________ (operate) on him.
3. Life-support machines ____________________ (keep) David alive after the accident.
4. When the EMT paramedics arrived, David ____________________ (not breathe).
5. Clara ____________________ (assisting) David at the accident scene.
6. The hospital staff ____________________ (take) care of David at the hospital.
7. The doctor ____________________ (feed) David through a feeding tube.
8. The drunk man ____________________ (drink) alcohol all afternoon the day of the accident.
9. David's parents ____________________ (not sleep) at 11:00 PM when they received the call from the hospital.
10. David's family ____________________ (talk) about what to do with his organs.
11. The hospital staff was looking for David's identification while Clara ____________________ (speak) to the doctor.
12. Life support machines ____________________ (help) David to stay alive.

Reading 2 We Have a Donor!

Before You Read

▸EXERCISE 11

A. Discuss these questions with a partner or a small group.

1. What is an organ transplant?
2. Do you think organ transplants are a good idea? Why or why not?
3. How can people make arrangements to donate their organs?
4. Do you want to donate your organs when you die?
5. Who should receive organ transplants, young people or older people?
6. Do you think organs should be free for everyone?

B. Write the antonym for the underlined word.

1. He is a sickly person. ________________
2. She is living with her illness. ________________
3. My friend has left the hospital. ________________
4. He has diseased kidneys. ________________
5. The operation was a failure. ________________

▸EXERCISE 12 Look at the pictures and write the correct letter next to each sentence.

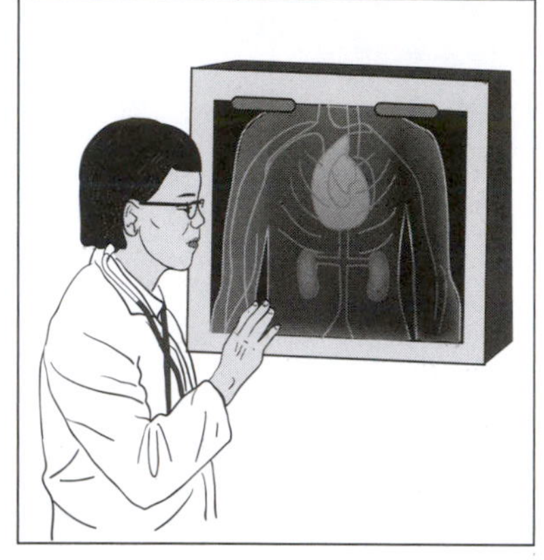

A.

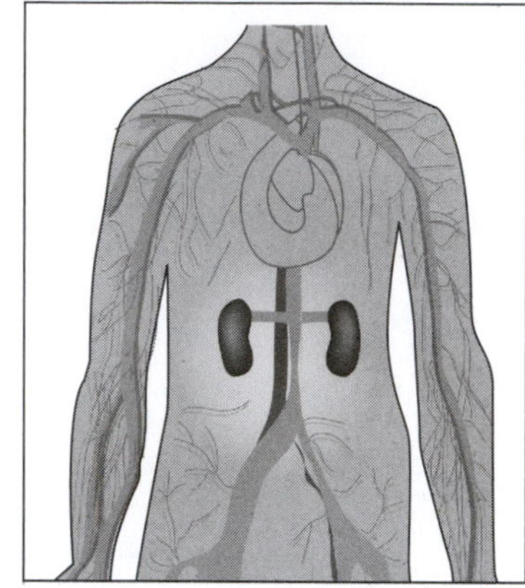

B.

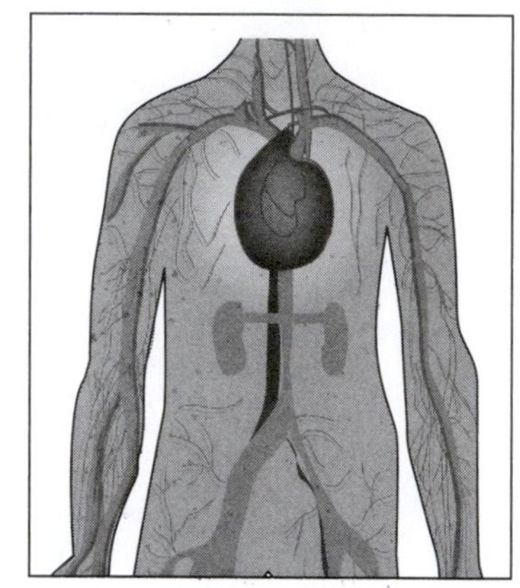

C.

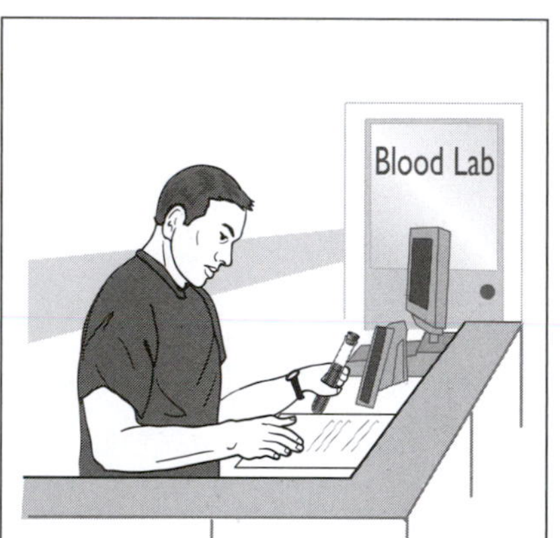

D.

E.

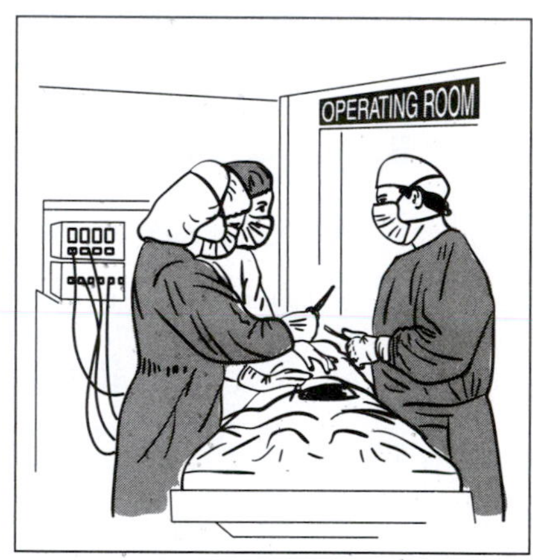

F.

1. David's blood and José's blood are compatible. ______
2. The operation takes fifteen hours. ______
3. José has heart disease. ______
4. José needs a kidney transplant. ______
5. David's tissue and José's tissue are compatible. ______
6. David's heart and kidneys are healthy. ______

▸EXERCISE 13 What word from "Words from the Reading" means the same as the underlined words? Write it on the line.

1. A person who gives or donates an organ. ____________________
2. A person who receives an organ. ____________________
3. To move organs from one person to another. ____________________
4. José has a very unhealthy heart. ____________________

Words from the Reading*

diseased **recipient**
donor **transplant**

*Your teacher can help you understand these words and others listed at the end of the chapter and on the Web site at http://esl.college.hmco.com/students.

▸EXERCISE 14 Scan the reading and answer the questions.

1. What is José's medical problem?

____

2. What difficult decision do David's parents need to make?

____

3. How will this decision affect José?

____

Read to find out about organ donors, recipients, and transplants.*

We Have a Donor!

José is forty-two years old, and he has had kidney and heart disease for ten years. He has a wife and two young children, but he has not worked for several years because of his physical condition. His doctors say that he is terminally sick but can live if he has a kidney and heart transplant. José has always been less healthy than most people his age, and now he is dying. His physical condition has gotten more serious in the last six months. He has stayed in the hospital this time for two months in intensive care.

*Related classes to take or visit: anatomy and physiology, nursing.

He has been on the organ donor recipient list for two years but has not found a donor. His diseased **kidneys** and heart have gotten weaker, so life-support machines have kept him alive for the last month.

José's doctors have looked for a younger donor without success until now. They found out about David as a possible donor, so they have spoken to David's doctor about José. José's doctors have told David's doctor that José has only a few months to live. David's parents know their son is dying, and David's doctor has spoken to David's parents about José's condition. David's parents have decided to give José life and hope. They have given legal **permission** to donate David's **organs** to José because David did not leave a will or an organ donor ID card with his driver's license. They think it is the **appropriate** decision. José's family knows that David's parents have made a difficult and generous decision, and they are very grateful.

The doctors say that it will be possible to transplant David's healthy organs into José. The doctors and the laboratory have done the proper tests, and they say that José's and David's blood and tissue are compatible. The transplant operation lasts fifteen hours and is more difficult and longer than expected. The doctors have taken David's strong kidneys and heart and transplanted them into José. David's family is sad, but they are excited for José. He will now live a more enjoyable life with his family. David's parents know that the organ **donation** was correct. David is now dead, but his heart and kidneys are alive in José.

appropriate	suitable, proper
donation	a gift or contribution
kidney	an abdominal organ that maintains the proper amount of water in the body and filters out wastes from the bloodstream in the form of urine
organ	an internal part of the body such as the heart, lungs, kidneys, and liver
permission	consent, authorization

Comprehension

▸EXERCISE 15 Complete the sentence with the main idea for each paragraph.

Paragraph 1: José is a young man who

____.

Paragraph 2: José's physicians have

____.

Paragraph 3: José's doctors say

____.

▸EXERCISE 16 Circle the letter of the correct answer.

1. José is terminally _____ and is in _____.
   a. dying; the hospital b. healthy; at home c. sick; intensive care
2. José's heart and kidneys are in serious _____.
   a. condition b. machines c. recipient
3. José has not had a _____ in _____ years.
   a. child; several b. disease; two c. job; several
4. With a kidney and heart _____, José can live a better life.
   a. transplant b. brain c. hope
5. José is terminally sick because of _____ kidneys and heart.
   a. old b. healthy c. diseased
6. After the transplant operation, José will _____ and David will _____.
   a. die; live b. live; die c. live; be healthier
7. The doctors and laboratory say that their tissue and blood are _____.
   a. weak b. incompatible c. compatible
8. David's family gives legal _____ for the transplant.
   a. donor b. permission c. will
9. David did not have a _____ or an organ donor _____.
   a. ID card; license b. permit; ID card c. will; ID card
10. José is the _____, and David is the _____.
    a. donor; recipient b. recipient; donor c. the victim; the donor
11. The parents have given legal _____ before the organ donation.
    a. permit b. permissions c. permitted
12. The doctors and lab have done the _____ tests.
    a. appropriate b. improper c. difficult

▶EXERCISE 17 Read the questions and answer them orally with your teacher. Then answer the questions orally with a classmate. At home, write the answers for homework. Answer in complete sentences.

About the Reading

1. Why is José terminally sick and in intensive care? ______________________________

   ____

2. What have José's doctors been looking for? ______________________________

   ____

3. How can David's parents help José? ______________________________

   ____

4. Who is the recipient of the healthy heart and kidneys? ______________________________

   ____

5. Why do the parents have to give legal permission for the organ donation? __________

   ____

6. How does David's family feel about José? ______________________________

   ____

What Do You Think?

7. Is taking organs from a dying person a good idea? Why or why not? ______________

   ____

8. Do you want a life-support machine for you? Why or why not? ______________

   ____

9. Do you have an "organ donor ID card" with your driver's license? ______________

   ____

10. What do you think should happen to the drunk man who hit David? ______________

    ____

Vocabulary Practice

▶EXERCISE 18 Complete each sentence with a word from the box.

compatible	donor	recipient	donate	grateful
organs	diseased	transplanted	permission	decision
disease	transplant	younger	generous	

1. According to the lab, José and David's blood and tissue were ____________.
2. David's family has given legal ____________ for the organ donation.
3. David's family wanted to ____________ David's organs to José.
4. Lungs, the liver, kidneys, and the heart are internal ____________.
5. I believe an organ ____________ ID card is a wonderful idea.
6. The patient who receives the new organ is the ____________.
7. José's heart and kidneys were so ____________ that he only had a short time to live.
8. If I am in an accident, I don't think I want my organs ____________ into another person.
9. José and his wife are very ____________ about David's parents' generosity.
10. David's parents made a very painful but appropriate ____________.
11. The doctors have looked for a ____________ donor.
12. David's parents have been very ____________ to José.
13. The ____________ operation lasted many hours.
14. José has a serious kidney ____________.

►EXERCISE 19 Complete each sentence with a verb from the box. Note that past participles in the irregular present perfect tense are irregular.

have given	have taken	have thought	has been
has had	has died	has said	have spoken
have told	has become	has done	has kept

1. David's parents ___*have given*___ legal permission for the transplant.
2. José ____________ diseased kidneys and heart for ten years.
3. David ____________ on life-support machines for over a week.
4. José's doctors ____________ to David's doctor about the organ donation.
5. David's parents ____________ about turning off the life-support machines, but it is a difficult decision.
6. David's doctor ____________ there is no hope for David.
7. The doctors ____________ (take) David's healthy organs from his body for the transplant operation to give to José.
8. David ____________, but his organs will live in José.
9. José's physical condition ____________ worse during the last month.
10. David's doctors ____________ his parents the bad news.
11. David's parents ____________ the correct thing with their son's organs.
12. A life support machine ____________ David alive for a while.

▸EXERCISE 20 Write the meaning of the underlined words using the prefix indicated.

Use the prefix *un-* (not).

1. Clara's job is not interesting sometimes. *uninteresting*
2. He is not excited about his new career. ____________
3. Her job is not enjoyable at times. ____________
4. The victim was not conscious. ____________
5. They were not decided about the donation. ____________
6. David's operation was not successful. ____________
7. I was not convinced about the operation. ____________
8. It was not an expected accident. ____________
9. José is not a healthy man. ____________

Use the prefix *in-* (not).

10. His decision was not appropriate. *inappropriate*
11. Her solution was not correct. ____________
12. Many donors' tissue was not compatible. ____________
13. He was not competent on the job. ____________
14. The life support machines were not effective. ____________
15. Some patients are not flexible. ____________
16. He is not a competent doctor. ____________
17. The paperwork is not complete. ____________

Reading Charts and Graphs

▶EXERCISE 21

A. Study the statistics about deaths and injuries caused by drunk driving.

Deaths and Injuries Caused by Alcohol in the United States in 2002

17,419	total alcohol-related fatalities
41%	of all fatalities are alcohol-related
1 person	number of people killed every 30 seconds
258,000	total people injured in these accidents
1 person	number of people injured every 2 minutes
1.4 million	total people arrested in the United States for driving under the influence of alcohol
1 driver	out of every 137 drivers is arrested for driving under the influence of alcohol

*U.S. Department of Transportation, National Commission on Drunk Driving, October 2003.

B. Answer the questions about the statistics.

1. What was the total number of people killed in alcohol-related accidents in 2002?

   ____

2. How many people died every thirty seconds from these accidents?

   ____

3. How many people were injured in 2002 due to alcohol-related accidents?

   ____

4. How many people were arrested for driving under the influence of alcohol?

   ____

5. How many people were injured every two minutes in alcohol-related traffic accidents in 2002? ____________________

6. What do you think should happen to drunk drivers who kill another person in a traffic accident? ____

   ____

7. What do you think is the solution to drinking and driving? ____________________

   ____

Expansion Activities

▸ Activity 1 Crossword Puzzle *Complete the puzzle using the clues provided.*

Across

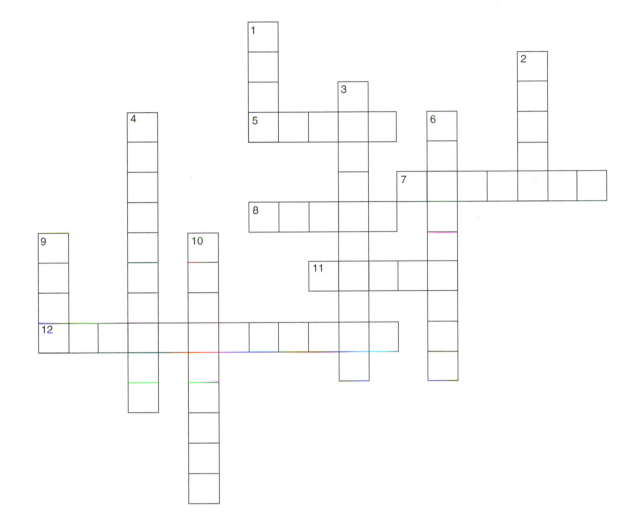

5. A person who donates organs
7. Antonym for *sick*
8. Antonym for *illegal*
11. Synonym for *correct*
12. Antonym for *naturally*

Down

1. Antonym of *alive*
2. José has a diseased ______ and kidneys.
3. David and José's blood is ______.
4. Emergency medical people
6. Synonym for *surgery*
9. David is in a ______ after the accident.
10. Person who gets organs

▸ Activity 2 Organ Donor ID Card *People can fill out organ donor forms when they obtain or renew a driver's license. Complete the sample organ donor form for practice.*

Uniform Donor Card

I, ________________________, have spoken to my family about organ and tissue donation. The following people have witnessed my commitment to be a donor. I wish to donate the following:

☐ any needed organs and tissue,

☐ only the following organs and tissue: ______________

Donor Signature: ______________________________

Date: ______________________________

Witness: ______________________________

Witness: ______________________________

Next of Kin: ______________________________

Telephone: (_____)______________________________

Vocabulary List

Adjectives
alive
appropriate
brain-dead
compatible
contagious
critical
dead
diseased
drunk
generous
grateful
healthy
intensive
legal
proper
rewarding
sick
stressful
tragic
unconscious
unsuccessful

Adverbs
naturally
normally
sadly
terminally

Nouns
accident
backboard
care
coma
CPR (cardiopulmonary resuscitation)
donation
donor
driver
emergency room
EMT paramedic
heart
hope
injury/injuries
intensive care
kidney
life-support machine
operation
organ
organ donation
permission
recipient
staff
stretcher
tissue
transplant
victim
witness
X-ray

Verbs—Present Tense
breathe
check
donate
keep
recover
transplant

Verbs—Past Tense
assessed
been
expected
loaded
provided
remained
responded
rushed
thought

Past Progressive
was bleeding
was giving
was not breathing
was not responding
were also keeping
were assisting
were feeding
were helping

Present Perfect Irregular
has been
has given
has gotten
has had
has spoken
have done
have kept
have made
have thought
have told

If you want to review vocabulary and complete additional activities related to this chapter, go to the *Read to Succeed 2* Web site at http://esl.college.hmco.com/students.

Appendix

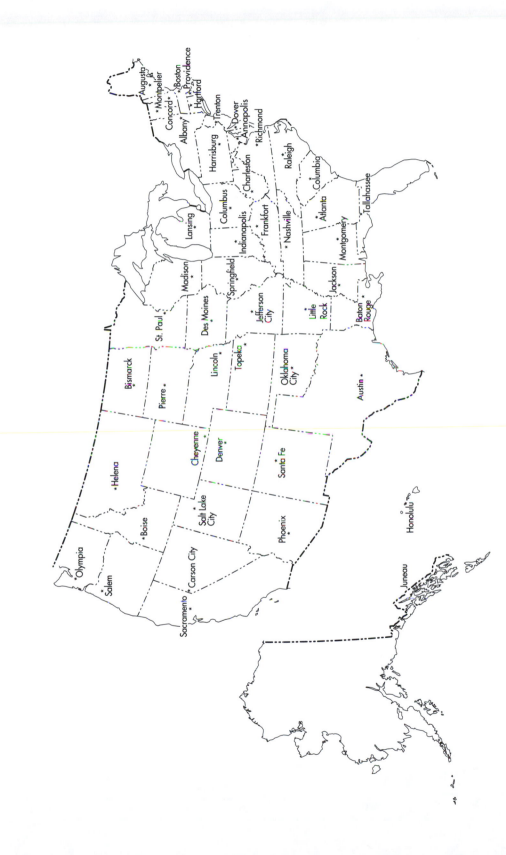

United States Map

World Map

Arctic Ocean
Russia
Mongolia
China
Bhutan
Bangladesh
Myanmar
Laos
Thailand
Vietnam
Kampuchea
Malaysia
Brunei
Singapore
Indonesia
N. Korea
S. Korea
Japan
Taiwan
Philippines
Guam
Palau
Micronesia
Marshall Islands
Papua New Guinea
Solomon Islands
Vanuatu
Fiji
Samoa Islands
Tonga
New Caledonia
Kiribati
French Polynesia
Australia
New Zealand
Pacific Ocean
Canada
U. S. A.
Mexico
Cuba
The Bahamas
Haiti
Dom. Rep.
Belize
Honduras
Jamaica
Guatemala
El Salvador
Nicaragua
Costa Rica
Panama
Guyana
Venezuela
Suriname
French Guiana
Colombia
Ecuador
Peru
Brazil
Bolivia
Chile
Paraguay
Argentina
Uruguay
Falkland Islands
South Georgia Island
Greenland
Iceland
Atlantic Ocean
Arctic Ocean
Norway
Sweden
Finland
Russia
Denmark
Estonia
Latvia
Lithuania
Ireland
Neth.
U. K.
Belgium
LUX.
Germany
Poland
Belarus
Czech
Slovakia
Ukraine
France
Switz.
Austria
Hungary
Moldova
Slovenia
Romania
Italy
Bosnia
Croatia
Montenegro
Serbia
Macedonia
Bulgaria
Albania
Greece
Portugal
Spain
Kazakhstan
Uzbekistan
Kyrgyzstan
Georgia
Armenia
Azerbaijan
Turkmenistan
Tajikistan
Turkey
Cyprus
Syria
Lebanon
Israel
Jordan
Iraq
Iran
Afghanistan
China
Nepal
Pakistan
India
Sri Lanka
Kuwait
Qatar
U. A. E.
Saudi Arabia
Oman
Yemen
Morocco
Tunisia
Canary Islands
Western Sahara
Algeria
Libya
Egypt
Mauritania
Mali
Niger
Chad
Sudan
Eritrea
Djibouti
Somalia
Senegal
Gambia
Guinea Bissau
Guinea
Burkina
Benin
Nigeria
Ghana
Ivory Coast
Togo
Cameroon
Sierra Leone
Liberia
African Republic
Ethiopia
Equatorial Guinea
Sao Tome & Principe
Congo
Gabon
Uganda
Kenya
Rwanda
Burundi
Tanzania
Angola
Zambia
Mozambique
Malawi
Zimbabwe
Namibia
Botswana
Madagascar
Swaziland
South Africa
Lesotho
Indian Ocean